WHAT READERS ARE SAYING

In "Random Reflections," Lois Schaffer shares personal stories that are life affirming and inspiring. Lois tells truly remarkable stories with modesty, humor and, most of all, with great love. Everyone should have a friend like Lois in their life. After reading this book, Lois will be a friend that you will remember and cherish.

—Robert Zimmerman, Co-founder ZE Creative Communications

Lois Schaffer's "Random Reflections" are touching, sentimental, inspirational, and eminently relevant to the world today. These musings by one of today's most impactful yet humble social activists reflect Lois' deep and abiding wisdom, cultivated through a lifetime of experiences with politics, family, love, loss, and changing the world.

—Rabbi A. Brian Stoller, Senior Rabbi, Temple Beth-El of Great Neck, New York

In "Random Reflections," Lois Schaffer has strung together a veritable necklace of some of the unexpected encounters and most precious moments of her life. These captivating vignettes will charm you, surprise you, touch you, and ultimately prod you to recall those encounters and people connections that have defined your own life experience. This volume reminds us to view each day as a new adventure.

—Thomas P. DiNapoli, New York State Comptroller

This is a joyous, rangy collection of remembrances from a life well lived. Lois's appetite for life, her energy, and her deep personal connection to dance are evident throughout these *pages. The writings about Martha Graham and the great Graham artist Pearl Lang are all the more potent for the embodied understanding she brings to these rare memories.*

—Janet Eilber, Artistic Director Martha Graham Dance Company.

random reflections

Encounters That Shape Us and the Invisible Threads That Bind Us

lois a. schaffer

Random Reflections

Copyright © 2025 by Lois Schaffer

All rights reserved.

Published by Red Penguin Books

Bellerose Village, New York

ISBN

Digital 978-1-63777-758-9

Print 978-1-63777-759-6

No part of this book may be reproduced in any form or by any electronic or mechanical means, including information storage and retrieval systems, without written permission from the author, except for the use of brief quotations in a book review.

DAVID

At the very outset of the foregoing essays, it is fitting and proper that an introduction be devoted to my husband, David.

The reasons are manifold. First, to avoid repetition of being referred to as "my husband, David." Second, to acknowledge his connection to many of these reflections. Third, to underscore the fact that these reflections would never have occurred if it hadn't been for him.

Throughout his lifetime, David has distinguished himself as a respected attorney and judge. He is admired for his infinite wisdom combined with a great sense of humor, a blend of heart and soul, and unsurpassed as a father, grandfather, great-grandfather, my husband and friend.

It is with abiding love and appreciation that I gratefully honor and highlight his association with these reflections and my life.

CONTENTS

Introduction	ix
1. ALL QUIET ON THE WESTERN FRONT, UNTIL	1
2. ETERNAL MEMORIES OF THE ETERNAL CITY	4
3. GLOBAL REFLECTIONS	8
4. THE LION KING	13
5. YOU CAN'T ALWAYS GET WHAT YOU WANT	18
6. BOOKSHOP REFLECTIONS	22
7. "MOVEMENT IS THE ESSENCE OF LIFE"	29
8. DANCING IN DANBURY	33
9. MARTHA GRAHAM	40
10. A SPECIAL RELATIONSHIP	46
11. UNORTHODOX PAIRINGS	55
12. DANCING FOR LIFE	61
13. SUSIE	67
14. EXERCISE: ITS UPS AND DOWNS	71
15. COINCIDENCE OR UNKNOWN FORCE?	78
16. ELLIOT FINEMAN	82
17. MY FRIENDSHIP WITH RUTH BADER GINSBURG	87
18. RABBI SUSAN TALVE	95
19. JILL SCHUPP	102
20. THE HEALER	107
21. WHAT GOES AROUND COMES AROUND	116
22. THE CIRCLE OF LIFE	120
Acknowledgments	123
AUTHOR'S NOTE	125
Also by Lois Schaffer	129

INTRODUCTION

"Life is not what one lived, but what one remembers and one remembers it."
Gabriel Garcia Marquez

Dear Reader:

This is not a memoir. Rather, it is a collection of experiences, reflections that have enriched my life.

One of the definitions in the dictionary regarding the word "reflection" is "giving serious thought or consideration."

Reflection can be attributed to both the tangible and intangible experience. I believe we all derive satisfaction from reminders of the moments that highlight the more meaningful aspects of our lives.

Tangible reflections include a variety of modes. Some people take photos or create videos or make voice recordings. Others will collect a souvenir from an event or a place they have visited. Still others will write songs, a symphony, an opera, poetry, or a novel, paint a picture, or create a ballet. In essence, the people making these reflections all serve to share something with others that has had a personal significance in their lives or highlight a memory they wish to maintain for their own consideration.

Of the intangible reflection, as a member of the Jewish community, I must mention Yom Kippur. While it is the day of atonement, the holiest day in Judaism, it is the quintessential example of reflection.

The question here moves beyond whether it is a tangible or intangible reflection. The real question is what was the result? Did it elicit a smile? A tear, perhaps? Was there anything that made this reflection a cause for change?

The following essays comprise my tangible means for reflection. They include places, people, and events that keep reverberating within my brain attendant with a strong desire to share them.

Some include recognizable names or places, others do not. Some are endowed with humor; others are filled with pathos. For me, they are worthy of retention for purposes of contemplation, personal growth, and sharing–reflections.

May this collection inspire you to reflect and recognize your own personal experiences and how you acknowledge them.

1

ALL QUIET ON THE WESTERN FRONT, UNTIL

"Never underestimate the heart of a champion."
Doc Rivers

The year was 1986.

David and I were guests at an elegant resort in Southern California. It was a combined business trip and vacation when David was the general counsel for the Avis Rent-A-Car corporation.

During our free time, we relaxed on chaise lounges by the pool.

The general environment was soothing: the baby blue skies, the sunny day, the dry Southern California air, and the ability to read without interruption were most welcome. The only annoyance was the sound of rock music coming from a distance.

David asked, "Isn't that music a little loud?"

"Yes, definitely," I replied.

With that I decided I wasn't going to tolerate the intrusion and chose to do something about it. Getting up from my chaise, I walked over to the area where the sound was coming from.

In short order, I found the culprit. He was a young African American, with a long lean body and enviable muscular physique. Looking at him, I concluded that he was an athlete. The well-built gentleman was sitting with his eyes closed listening to the music. I almost did not have the heart to intrude on his reverie, but enough was enough. I gently tapped him on the shoulder, and he opened his eyes.

I asked him as politely as possible, "I'm sorry to bother you, but could you please turn that music down?"

"Sure, no problem," he replied and quickly lowered the volume.

Thanking him, I returned to my chaise and continued reading, having accomplished my mission.

Subsequently, David went for a walk. He returned with the biggest smile on his face.

"What are you smiling about?" I asked.

"Do you know the identity of the guy you asked to lower the music?"

Before I could respond, David blurted out, "Marvelous Marvin Hagler."

"His name is Marvelous?"

"Yeah, that's his nickname."

"And whatever makes him so marvelous?"

"Just the world's middleweight boxing champion, that's all. He's training here in Southern California for his next bout with John Mugabi in Las Vegas."

"Really? No wonder he looked like an athlete to me."

Still smiling, David and I looked at one another. Here I was talking to a celebrity and didn't have a clue. We both burst out laughing at the turn of events.

We came across Marvelous Marvin several times during our stay at the resort. We saw him jogging alone, walking with crew members, carrying his gear and other times having breakfast by himself in the coffee shop.

My encounters with Marvelous Marvin quickly disabused me of my perception of boxing champions and superstar athletes as being catered to by an entourage of aides, spear carriers, and hangers on. With Marvin, they were conspicuous by their absence. Marvelous Marvin appeared to be a private person although rightfully captured by the spotlight.

Certainly, his kind response to me was indicative of his nature.

His passing in 2021 was all too soon. He was only sixty-six years old, but a true credit in the sports world and humanity.

In retrospect, I was proud to have met him, even if briefly, and I regard the annoyance of the invasive music as a gift that initiated an encounter with a wonderful human being.

2
ETERNAL MEMORIES OF THE ETERNAL CITY

"Rome was a poem pressed into service as a city."
Anatole Broyard

Memories of a very special trip to Rome still resonate with me decades after my visit to the Eternal City. The year was 1968, and it was my first trip abroad. Just the thought of experiencing a different culture with people of different backgrounds elicited boundless anticipation and excitement.

David and I were born and bred in the United States. Just two Jews who grew up in the Bronx. As we matured, learning about various cultures and traveling abroad intrigued us.

That reality was made possible when David was hired as general counsel at Avis Rent-A-Car, an international organization whose parent company was Chrysler. In addition to the opportunities to visit various parts of the world, our travels also initiated friendships with people within the United States and abroad. It is interesting to note that we have maintained some of those friendships to this day.

The purpose of this trip was to attend an international Avis convention that would connect us socially and professionally with Europeans and people from different parts of the United States.

Prior to our departure we had dinner with a friend and told him about our upcoming trip.

Our friend listened and delightedly explained, "A Roman friend of mine is a Jesuit priest who can arrange for a Papal audience." He quickly added, "It doesn't mean a private audience, but one that is in the Basilica that the Pope conducts about twice a week with hundreds of people in attendance."

"Sounds great, anyway," we said.

Neither smartphones, nor computers existed in the '60s, so consequently our friend reached into his jacket and took out his pen and a piece of paper, as he continued to speak, "I'll be in touch with my friend and tell him to expect your call when you arrive. This is his phone number," he said as he wrote down the information and handed it to us.

We called the priest upon our arrival and met with him at a church in the heart of a lovely neighborhood in Rome.

The priest was an elderly tall, lean man with sparkling blue eyes. Our conversation was made easy by his excellent command over the English language. We chatted for a while and shared how we just happened to have dinner with our mutual friend and how grateful we were that he had connected us to the priest.

Without further ado, he said, "I have six tickets" and inserted them into an envelope. "Present them when you arrive at the Basilica and someone will direct you to your seats."

After thanking the priest profusely, David and I walked out of the church and hailed a taxi back to our hotel. We felt as though our feet weren't touching the ground, so enthralled were we at our good fortune.

"Remarkable," David exclaimed, as we rode in the taxi. "Six tickets!" Now, who can we invite to join us?"

"Good question. Who can we ask that would be most appropriate?"

David thought for a moment. "What about Ron?"

"Good idea," I said, "because he is also a Jew and I think would especially appreciate experiencing this opportunity. Who else do you think we can include?"

"How about Keith?"

"Keith," of course.

Keith was a young London resident and Avis' financial advisor. David and Keith had a lot in common due to their legal and financial backgrounds. "He would be thrilled to attend the audience," David added.

Then David blurted out, "The two Irishmen, Mike and Sean."

"That's a super idea."

"Let's go find those guys and invite them," David said the minute the taxi dropped us off at our hotel.

Later we learned that Chrysler was also distributing tickets for the audience. However, there was a caveat. Those who would be eligible to secure a ticket had to be part of the Chrysler/Avis organizational upper echelon and Catholic.

While Mike and Sean were Catholic, they did not qualify because they were not included in the organization's upper rank.

The rest of us fit neither category.

I vividly recall the six of us arriving at St. Peter's at the Basilica. The first glimpse of the building in all its overwhelming beauty, the grandeur and vastness left us speechless. Soon, we were ushered to our seats close to where the Pope would deliver his address.

As we waited for the service to begin, we kept smiling at one another. It was almost as if we knew what each of us was thinking. It was a communal disbelief that we were having such a momentous experience.

We then noticed a large group of people entering the nave. It was the Chrysler/Avis contingent composed of both the corporation's Catholics and upper echelon employees.

We watched as they approached us, nodded in recognition, and observed as they continued walking all the way to the back of the nave.

Later, we learned that the seating in the Basilica was determined by one's importance. It was the Jesuit priest who had made it possible for our seating up front. David and I chuckled that here we were, two Jews from the Bronx, who had managed to secure better seats than the 'big shots.'

While Ron and Keith derived a special feeling from this experience, Mike and Sean were over the moon. They could not stop hugging us after the service was over and practically davened whenever they saw us in endless genuine gratitude for having made it possible for them to see the Pope.

More than fifty years have lapsed since that memorable day. I've never forgotten the joy we felt and our added pleasure making it possible for others to have this unforgettable experience. I've always wondered whether that experience still resonates with those who accompanied us on that day, particularly Mike and Sean as it does with David and me.

3

GLOBAL REFLECTIONS

Strength lies in differences, not similarities.
Stephen R. Covey

The pros and cons of diversity, equity, and inclusion (DEI) have recently been highlighted in the news. Negatively, DEI can be viewed as discrimination and injustice. I have always focused on the beauty of differences and the equality of the human condition while welcoming others who are not like me into my life.

DEI emphasizes human values and identity.

David and I lived DEI decades before it became a prominent topic of our national discussion. During David's seventeen-year tenure as general counsel for Avis, which was an international organization, we often connected with diverse people from all over the globe at conventions, combined business meetings and receptions in the United States and abroad. These individuals represented many different cultures, spoke different languages, had a strong command of the English language and were interesting as well as delightful to be with.

Our trips to California and Rome were representative of many other enlightening travel experiences for Avis. In truth, all of those trips were noteworthy in terms of the sites we visited, the people we met, and the fun we had.

Most important, they were a first-hand blending of DEI and our adventure-seeking selves.

There was one time, however, when a four-day corporate convention was scheduled to be held in New York City instead of abroad.

We live in Great Neck, just over the city line and an easy trip to and from midtown Manhattan. Consequently, David and I suggested to Avis' president the idea of hosting a dinner reception in our home one of the evenings. Our plan was to serve an American-style dinner to the Avis associates who would be traveling to New York from foreign countries.

That suggestion led to one of the most rewarding experiences of our lives.

Avis personnel sent invitations to all those who were planning to attend the convention.

The days leading up to the dinner at our home were filled with several activities including ordering tables and chairs from a party rental company and preparing American dishes such as chili, mac and cheese and a chocolate ice-cream cake.

We learned that our guests were to include sixty-eight people from abroad.

The appointed day arrived. That evening, David and I stood at our doorway waiting for our guests. As expected, a large bus stopped in front of our home.

It was a remarkable sight as we watched scores of people representing various ethnicities quickly emerge from the bus.

We derived enormous pleasure as we greeted each person individually and were privileged to welcome them into our home.

David and I enthusiastically interacted with our guests during the cocktail hour. I heard what seemed to be an endless multitude of different languages spoken with intermittent, beautifully accented English.

Similarly, the dinner conversations were engaging, insightful and intellectually stimulating, accompanied by witnessing our guests appreciating the American-inspired meal we had prepared.

It was a thrilling and uplifting experience that would be a source of thoughtful reflection for years to come, even though at the time it seemed as if it had ended in a flash.

After saying goodbye, David and I stood at the door and watched as the bus pulled away from our home.

Thinking about the night some fifty years later, I recall the joyful camaraderie that characterized the interactions of the people in attendance. It exemplified the principles of Diversity, Equity, and Inclusion (DEI) an increasingly critical issue in contemporary society, affirming the equality of individuals irrespective of their ethnic background.

4
THE LION KING

If at first you don't succeed, try, try again."
William Edward Hickson

The *Lion King* opened on Broadway in 1997. Rachel, our 12-year-old granddaughter, was going to fly in to visit us from St. Louis for ten days at the end of the summer just prior to when the Fall semester began at school.

Rachel was eager to see *The Lion King*, a shared excitement for all of us. The reviews were excellent, and tickets were difficult to get due to its popularity. Purchasing tickets for this Broadway production was even more of a challenge because our granddaughter was only going to be in New York for a brief ten-day period.

Reserving theater seats over the internet was not an option in 1997. The only means to purchase tickets were phone reservations or at the box office.

I had tried calling the box office several times but could not get tickets for the allotted time Rachel was going to be in New

York. I even drove into Manhattan from our home on Long Island and waited in long lines to try to purchase tickets. Each attempt was met with disappointment. Still, no tickets were available during the limited time they were needed.

I had an idea the night before I was going to pick Rachel up at the airport. Bake cookies.

David watched me that evening and asked me why I was baking cookies.

I explained that perhaps it would give me a "leg up" to purchase tickets. While it might not produce the outcome I wanted, I thought it would be a nice thing to do. "After all," I said, "I've watched the ticket agents work long, hard hours and maybe the cookies would be a lovely gesture and a source of energy."

I recall David looking a little puzzled, but he smiled and said, "OK, I'll buy it."

"You know that I think outside the box."

"You sure do."

The cookies were baked. I put them in a tin with a note that included my contact information and my gift to the ticket agents for their enjoyment.

I drove to the airport the next day to pick Rachel up with the cookie tin securely placed on the back seat.

"What's that?" Rachel said, as got into the car and pointed to the cookie tin.

I explained that we were going to drive into the city and go to *The Lion King* box office to try to purchase tickets for a performance while she was visiting.

"So, what's with the cookies?"

"I thought that would set me apart from everyone else because tickets for this show are so difficult to get and you are only here for a short time."

"Grandma," she said, "you're bribing them?"

I couldn't help but laugh. "No, I look at it as something that is thoughtful and different, and the ticket agents would remember me."

Rachel rolled her eyes.

"We could drive into the city now and then meet Poppy for dinner."

As we drove into the city, Rachel kept repeating, "It's a bribe, I know it's a bribe."

We parked the car near the theater and walked to the box office. All the while, I held onto the cookie tin.

We entered the theater lobby. Miraculously, there was no other person waiting online to buy tickets. Rachel headed for the nearest corner with both hands trying to hide her face.

When the ticket agent spotted me, he asked, "Did you bring me food?"

"I did. Please enjoy these cookies," and handed the tin to him. "You see that kid standing in the corner? That's my granddaughter. She is too embarrassed that I'm giving these cookies to you."

The ticket agent smiled, opened the tin, and took out a cookie. "This is delicious."

"Thank you," I answered. "They're my family's favorite."

"These are especially good," the agent added.

"Now about tickets to a performance. I know you must hear stories from people trying to buy tickets to a popular show. This is mine. I have tried to buy tickets several times with no luck for the specific time they were for only ten days. And that's the problem."

The ticket agent paused for a moment and typed something on his computer.

I have three tickets in the middle section of the theater. Two of them are together and one is in the same row but at the end of the row. The performance is in two days."

"I'll take them."

David and I decided we would switch seats during the intermission so that each of us would sit with Rachel.

We arrived at the theater anticipating a great performance and an usher directed us to our seats.

A gentleman was sitting in the middle next to our two seats and was reading the playbill. "Excuse me, sorry for the interruption. Are you alone?" I asked.

"Yes," he said.

Pointing to the end of the row, I said, "You see that man sitting at the end of the row? That's my husband. My granddaughter and I would be so grateful if we could sit together. Would you mind switching your seat with him?"

Without any hesitation, he replied, "Of course," and immediately stood up to switch seats.

Fast forward, twenty-six years. As great-grandparents we took our great granddaughter to see *The Lion King*.

Reflecting on my treks into the city twenty-six years earlier, again I personally drove into the city to buy tickets. After I purchased them, I said to the ticket agent, "Let me tell you a story about when my husband and I took her mother to see this production twenty-six years ago."

I believe that baking cookies gave me that advantage.

5
YOU CAN'T ALWAYS GET WHAT YOU WANT

"The best laid plans of mice and men often go awry."
Robert Burns

The word "cookies" can be defined in many ways. Most familiarly, the kind that is eaten. Then, there is the expression, "That's the way the cookie crumbles," which can be thought of as resigned disappointment over something that has reluctantly happened.

In our family, cookies, or more specifically baking cookies, have become a coded message for making a special connection with others.

This is the story.

Our daughter, Susie, may she rest in peace, was divorced and a single working mother.

From a young age, Susie's coordination, mobility, and athletic ability shone through. Consequently, she chose a life of movement and trained to become a certified Pilates and Gyrotonic instructor.

Susie lived in St. Louis, and we live in New York where she grew up before moving away with her family and before becoming a mother.

Susie's Pilates and Gyrotonic certification process was scheduled to take place in Colorado over several school days and a weekend. She asked me to fly to St. Louis to take care of her three young children while she was away. Although her ex-husband lived in the same city, he was unavailable to help during the five days Susie would be out of town.

It was always a joy to spend time with the grandchildren. Regrettably, David was working and could not accompany me. He would be missed, but even so, I looked forward to spending time with the children.

During our time together, the four of us had great fun, including dinners at some of the children's favorite restaurants where I even permitted them to have the occasional extra dessert.

The days flew by. I was kept on-the-go with their schedules at school and their many extra-curricular activities.

On Saturday morning, the doorbell rang. It was the children's father. He explained that his work schedule had changed, and he was now available to take the children to his home for the remainder of the time their mother was away.

I was slightly taken aback as he hadn't gotten in touch with me to let me know of this change of plans.

I called Susie to tell her I was contemplating returning to New York ahead of time due to this unexpected change. Her response was that my leaving would not be her first choice, but that after all, her ex-husband was the father, and he had every right to take the children back to his home.

The situation had its upside. I would be going home to my husband.

The children left with their father. I quickly packed and called a taxi to take me to the airport. From previous experience, I knew that the airport was not generally crowded on Saturdays, so I thought I could easily fly standby–that is, having previously paid for a ticket on another flight, I could secure an empty seat just before departure at no extra cost.

I spoke to a flight attendant and inquired about the possibility of a standby seat. While there were indeed fewer travelers on Saturday, there were also fewer flights, consequently fewer available seats. The attendant informed me that flying standby would not be an option.

I asked the flight attendant if I could speak to the airport manager.

An official, wearing his airport uniform, appeared within a short time and introduced himself as "David."

My eyes lit up, thinking this was a way to "break the ice," I said, "Nice name. I'm partial to that name because it's also my husband's name, and I would like to get home to him."

I explained that my visit to St. Louis had been cut short, and I was now trying to return home as a standby instead of on my scheduled flight, which was the next day.

David listened, pausing for a moment, and then he uttered, "Sure, I can get you on this flight, but it would require you to purchase another ticket or use your frequent flyer miles."

"How much would a new ticket cost?" I asked.

I was aghast when I heard the amount.

"And what would it require to use my mileage?"

Again, it was astronomical.

"Is the flight fully booked?"

"No, it is not."

"I'm sorry, but I think that's unfair. Why can't I fly standby at no extra cost if the flight is not fully booked? After all, I bought a ticket for tomorrow's flight."

I could see that David was becoming impatient with me. Finally, he said, "Sorry, ma'am," turned on his heels, and briskly walked away.

Having been denied the opportunity to board the flight, I hailed a taxi back to Susie's home.

As I rode in the taxi, all I could think of was how wrongly I'd been treated and wondered why the airline would rather have an empty seat than one that was occupied. Resigned to my fate as I was, that familiar phrase "that's the way the cookie crumbles" felt appropriate.

As soon as the taxi dropped me off, I called David and related the whole unpleasant experience at the airport.

His immediate response was, "You should've baked cookies."

6
BOOKSHOP REFLECTIONS

"A room without books is like a body without a soul."
Cicero

Our family loves books. It's not an exaggeration to say that books stimulate the senses of hearing, sight and touch.

Hearing about a book, seeing words on the page, and holding a book give rise to a thought process that is without equal.

It must also be mentioned that the act of reading has, of late, taken on a different focus. Specifically, people now read books electronically: on tablets, smart phones, e-readers, and computers. This makes me wonder: How will you be reading *this* book? (But I digress.) While it might be more efficient, digital reading, sadly in my view, deprives book lovers of the tactile, timeless treasure of "curling up with a good book."

As an octogenarian, I prefer a "traditional" means of reading and have fond memories of independent bookshops that have inspired my love of books and the printed page.

While large chain bookshops have arisen and some have even disappeared, I am referring to the small bookshops that are now a rarity to the extent that even the word, "bookshop" seems quaint. The following is an account of two such bookshops, the Book Mark and Theodore's Books, that have made an impression on my life, one years ago and one today.

The Book Mark, which I remember well from my youth, was located in Queens and was in business from the 1940s to the 1970s. It was a popular store and had a wonderfully diverse collection of books, stationery, cards, and board games. The store was owned by two sisters, Rose and Esther Weiner. Both women were fun to talk to. They were warm, welcoming, and well read. Buying a book from their store, especially one as a gift, was an experience that was frequently based on "insider knowledge" because very often Rose and Esther would read books that arrived in their shop. As a result, their advice about a particular book would be based on their firsthand opinion in addition to publishers' blurbs and book reviews.

Two other people also worked in the store: Mr. Weiner, who was Rose and Esther's father, and an employee by the name of Agnes.

Mr. Weiner was a sweet, elderly gentleman who would occasionally help customers at the cash register; Agnes was a kind lady but more sharp, "businesslike," and was particularly focused on keeping the shop neat and clean.

Thanks to the Weiner sisters' hospitable nature, the shop became a "hangout" for people in the neighborhood and elsewhere who would drop in to have a chat with Rose, Esther, or Mr. Weiner and to some degree, Agnes, as well.

I lived in the shop's vicinity through high school and college and was among those who liked to stop by for a quick social visit.

After David and I married in 1957, we returned to the same general area when Susie was born in 1960.

Even as a toddler, Susie developed the same warm feeling about the shop that David and I had.

In her stroller, we would go for walks in the neighborhood. Her pronunciation of Esther, Rose, and Agnes's names was cute and funny. In her usage, they were Wose, Aster and Aganes. When she realized where we were on our walks, she would say, "Let's go visit Wose and Aster, but not Aganes."

Susie's attraction to Rose and Esther stemmed from the fact that they would read books to her whenever the shop was not too busy. Either of them would give her a big hug, put her on their lap and proceed to read a fun children's story, bringing joy to her from start to finish.

There was no doubt that Susie sensed their warmth, enmeshed in their undivided attention.

But Susie was always conscious of Agnes watching given her insistence on keeping the store organized.

There were instances when Susie would begin to handle the cards on the shelves. Agnes would gently admonish her, "Uh, uh, uh, you can look, but you can't touch."

Rose and Esther were quite subtle while handling a similar situation.

I remember an occasion when we were in the store to buy a birthday gift, and I was busy talking to Esther. Agnes was not working in the store that day. Three-year-old Susie was roaming around and reached out to one of the shelves holding cards, causing the cards to promptly fall to the floor.

As we saw the cards strewn about, Esther and I heard Susie say, "Uh, uh, uh, don't tell Aganes."

It was all Esther could do to keep from bursting out in laughter. Instead, sensitively stifling her impulse, she said to Susie, "I know it was an accident. Let's put the cards back together and I won't tell Agnes."

With that, it was Susie's turn to give Esther a big hug.

Moments like the ones involving the Weiner sisters still reverberate in my mind and continue to remain special more than sixty years later.

That was then, this is now.

My reference is to Theodore's Books in Oyster Bay, Long Island. It is another quintessentially small, independent bookstore and the brainchild of former congressman Steve Israel.

It felt like déjà vu when I first entered Theodore's immediately after its opening in November 2021. Taking its name from former president and Oyster Bay resident Theodore Roosevelt, it has a friendly environment, a well-stocked collection of greeting cards, and an extraordinary inventory of books.

Theodore's is reminiscent of the Book Mark in those exemplary ways, along with one difference. It is staffed by considerably more associates than its older counterpart. The employees, much like Rose and Esther before them, are knowledgeable and kind.

The gracious atmosphere at Theodore's, and my appreciation of it, are due to its source: Steve Israel.

Israel, an author of two highly acclaimed novels, a longstanding former member of the House of Representatives, and a former staff member of the American Jewish Congress, continues to reinvent himself as a catalyst on many levels.

Currently, he is the director of the non-partisan Institute of Politics and Global Affairs at Cornell University, while managing to keep a watchful eye on his latest preoccupation.

Israel sees a connection between his previous work in public service and current occupation as a passionate bookstore owner. He says, "You have to meet voters where they are. The same is true of our patrons."

And with regard to his staff at Theodore's, he thoughtfully expressed his organizational thinking. "Our booksellers aren't hired just to sell you a book, but to listen to your tastes and preferences."

His words illustrate an emphasis on both reaching out and inspiring others to embrace his strong belief in the pleasures of reading.

My first encounter with Steve Israel occurred during his inaugural congressional candidacy in 2001. I have come to admire his concern for others, including his constituents and now his bookshop customers ever since.

Perhaps even more important, as a survivor of gun violence, in addition to being a former constituent, I am indebted to him for his strong stance on gun-safety measures.

With his impressive credentials as a former congressman, a respected author, and an expert on global affairs, Israel brings to the bookstore's ownership a wide range of experience. His focus on outreach is demonstrated by his invitations to nationally known people active in the world of public affairs and the arts for interviews, lectures and book signings, as they share valuable ideas for the community and the world at large.

Since its inception, I have attended several book signings at Theodore's. These events attract people from many walks of life, often including children in the company of parents.

Visions of Rose and Esther resonate as I've watched Israel hug children who happen to be at the bookstore during those special events or with a family member buying a book during normal business hours.

While the Book Mark and Theodore's existed in different eras, both exemplified camaraderie and enrichment. Their presence was begun and sustained by their public-spirited owners who wished to inspire others and promote the appreciation of the unique mind-expanding wonder of reading.

It is my hope that this inspiration and appreciation will be passed on to the next generation.

While the world may be fast moving towards the idea of a more digital acceptance of books and reading, the fact remains that none can replace the feeling of the book in your hand, the long-forgotten dried flowers safely tucked away in pages, a reminder of good times and the warmth of the black letters on a fading yellow page. The Book Mark and Theodore's beautifully demonstrate how the past, present and future are so meaningfully intertwined in my life.

7
"MOVEMENT IS THE ESSENCE OF LIFE"

Bernd Heinrich

I have always put an emphasis on being physically active, a value that was first instilled in me by my parents.

The visual experience of watching bodies move through space is exciting whether it be sport related or dance.

In sports, one of the activities I appreciate most is basketball, not only because it is among the most graceful of athletic endeavors, but because my father played on the New York University basketball team.

It is interesting to note that my father's given name was Isadore but he was referred to by his friends as "Hawky." I once asked my mother about that discrepancy, "If Daddy's name is Isadore, why do people call him Hawky?"

My mother told me it was a shortened version of "Hawkeye," that was created by his friends because he was a prolific scorer and regarded as a "star" on his team.

Both of my parents had a powerful influence on my physical pursuits, placing a high value on movement in one form or another. My father's prowess on the basketball court was an incentive to me to lead an active life. However, it was my mother who was the dance enthusiast in the family, enrolling me in dance classes when I was ten years old and taking me to many dance concerts. Those experiences captured my interest in that particular form of movement that would manifest itself in a variety of ways later in life.

My everlasting connection to dance stems from the appreciation of its physicality and artistry. While I speak from personal experience, dance as an art form has universal appeal as a fluid means of human expression.

Dance, in its many forms, be it ballroom, tap, ballet, or modern, can increase strength and flexibility; improve heart rate, posture, balance and aerobic fitness all of which are important contributions to good health.

In whatever form it takes, dance is a joy to participate in and to watch flexible bodies stretch and navigate through space often with beautiful musical accompaniment.

All of that is not to mention how taking a dance class with other people can initiate a deep feeling of commonality.

In high school, instead of the required gym class, I was accepted into the dance department's program. The teacher was Mrs. Leahy, a former dancer, and a wonderful inspiration to her students who were fortunate enough to study under her.

To this day, I recall Mrs. Leahy and performing in a dance piece she choreographed for her students to one of Chopin's piano concertos. I vividly remember the pleasure I derived from her joyous choreography combined with Chopin's music, and the energizing effect the experience had on me as I danced with other students in the class.

After high school, I was accepted at Adelphi College, (now University) and chose dance as my major.

Entwined in my college experience was a figurative trip to the past and thoughts of my father owing to the New York Knickerbockers basketball team conducting their training camp at Adelphi.

Due to my father's history as a basketball player, the presence of the Knick's at the same school I was attending combined memory and moment in a way that seemed almost magical.

Adelphi's dance studio and running track were located upstairs in the gym building and could be entered from two swinging doors. The gym was downstairs, and on my way to and from a dance class, I would see these enormously tall men running from one end of the court to the other as they practiced their sport.

A lighthearted incident from those days remains etched in memory.

I was heading upstairs onto the running track on my way to a dance class and opened the swinging doors with my back. At that very moment, as I turned around, I walked directly into the navel of the famous Knicks player, Nat "Sweetwater" Clifton.

Gazing upward, I stopped cold in my tracks. It was like looking up at a mountain. As our eyes met, Clifton's reaction erupted in such a roar of laughter as we collided that I imagined seeing his tonsils.

After the initial reaction, I remember that we both stopped for a moment to take stock of the comical situation. However, just as quickly as it occurred, that is how quickly it ended. Sweetwater, in his polished athletic way, turned around and practically floated down the stairs to join his teammates as I continued to head towards my dance class.

Two people collided, sport and dance in spirit but blended in one metaphorical instance.

And so, contained within the following pages are cherished memories of my love of dance not just as an art form but as physical exercise.

8

DANCING IN DANBURY

"Everything is a learning experience."
Angus T. Jones

Kenmere Park was a summer vacation spot located on Lake Kenosia in Danbury, Connecticut, that was developed in the early 1900s. It grew to become a bungalow colony in the mid-1940s.

The colony was a popular destination for families who preferred to spend summers together in a country-like setting. It had a rustic feeling, nestled in the New England mountains, surrounded by stately trees and grassy lawns and situated on Lake Kenosia, which offered myriad opportunities for boating and fishing.

The bungalows were compact yet ample with one to three bedrooms, a kitchenette, a sitting area, and porches for vacationers to delightedly experience the natural beauty of the area. A clubhouse for community events, several tennis courts and a children's camp, Camp Kenmere, added to the appeal of the colony.

Lifelong friendships developed, with many families returning each summer and sharing stories of their respective lives. The women would organize games of Canasta or mahjong. The men would organize their own card games and schedule golf outings or tennis matches. Besides attending the camp, the children would play games of tag and hide and seek or would swim in the lake.

It was idyllic, a place where I enjoyed making new friends, and where I had the unexpected pleasure of using dance to open a whole new world of fun for myself and others.

During the summers of 1948 and 1949, my parents decided to rent a bungalow at Kenmere Park as a family.

Like the other families who had rented a cabin, we were going to spend the time together in this picturesque setting.

Unlike some families, my father was only going to be with my mother and me on weekends because he had to go to work.

The colony was roughly a two-hour drive from where we lived in Queens, New York. On Fridays, instead of going to the office, my father would drive to Danbury arriving that Friday morning, and then would drive back to New York the following Monday morning.

I vividly remember my mother waiting for his phone call on Monday to say that he had returned safely to New York.

While I missed seeing my father during the week, the days flew by because I was going to be quite occupied at camp.

Before camp started, I met Jack, the camp director. He learned that I was thirteen and would be fourteen in the fall. He seemed impressed that even at that tender age, I was a serious dance student. We realized that all the other children enrolled at the camp were eleven years old or younger. Reflecting on this, Jack suggested an approach that would take advantage of both my age and my dance training.

"You're too old to be a normal camper, but too young to be a regular counselor," he said. "How would you like to be a junior counselor, to assist our dance counselor?"

My eyes widened in excitement.

I was thrilled but felt a little nervous. It was somewhat scary for me, yet a chance for a new, interesting experience doing what I loved to do: dance. I remember sheepishly asking Jack whether he thought I could really do the job. "You'll be fine," he said. To make things even better, I was given a small stipend as a thank you.

So, for the next eight weeks I was employed as a junior counselor in dance.

I was feeling an equal sense of both trepidation and elation. As I look back on it now, all of the full-fledged counselors were in their 20s, and being a young teenager, I considered that to be "old."

The essence of this experience lay in the fact that I was welcomed with open arms, treated with respect, and included in their circle. It was flattering to connect with these people whom I considered to be so grown up, experienced and mature.

I remember the dance counselor; her name was Maya. She was very attractive and of American Indian heritage. Maya was a college graduate like the other counselors and had been teaching dance at Kenmere for several summers.

It was an exciting time supporting Maya in teaching the fifty or so children who were enrolled in the camp. As her assistant, I helped to demonstrate the many exercises and movements she taught. Unlike the ballet, tap, and modern dance classes I took at home, her classes included a number of movements from her native culture.

This schedule continued for the first four weeks of camp. However, one morning when I arrived at my usual spot to assist Maya, she was nowhere to be found. Just then, Jack arrived and came right over to me.

Hurriedly, he explained, "Maya left the camp last night and will not be returning."

"What happened?" I asked.

"We don't know, but we no longer have a dance counselor. How do you feel about assuming that role? I think you are capable of taking charge."

Again, I felt skittish yet exhilarated.

Trying to appear mature, I told Jack, "If you trust me, I'd love to do it. May I run back to my bungalow to tell my mom?"

"Do you have a dance session immediately scheduled?"

"No, I do not. I have an hour before a session with the nine-to eleven-year-olds."

"Good, then go. Tell your mom the news."

I remember starting to run back to my bungalow only to take a quick U-turn and run right back to ask Jack another question.

"What am I going to say to the campers?"

He quickly responded, "Don't be concerned. I will handle that. Just do what you have to do."

I was sorry Maya left but delighted to be given this special opportunity. With added energy, I raced through the grounds of the colony, burst into the door of our bungalow, and breathlessly told my mother the news.

After a loving, congratulatory hug and kiss, my mom ran to the phone and called my father at his office.

"Hawky, lovely news," she said, and shared the circumstances of this new development.

I could hear my father's reaction on the other end. He said, "I am so proud of her and know she can take on this job without question."

With newfound confidence, I hugged and kissed my mom and returned to the dance space to begin my first time, first day as dance counselor to the campers.

As I headed back to the camp, I thought that while I was not much older than these kids, I wanted to create an even balance between their age and mine. I thought about Maya and the movements she had taught but wanted to teach the kids some of the classical techniques I had learned. They were an energetic bunch, so I incorporated running, skipping and jumping into my teaching sessions to make the most of their boundless vitality.

It was in this manner that I continued to work with the children during the remaining four weeks of camp. Thankfully, I eased into my new role by the end of the first week.

That feeling was only heightened when parents of the campers who saw me would say, "My daughter (or son) loves your dance sessions. I have watched her (or him) when they do not see me doing some kind of movement that they learned from you."

Two weeks before camp ended, Jack announced that there was going to be a "gala night." To mark the end of summer camp, all of the children were invited to perform, whether it be to sing a song, play a piece on the piano, recite a poem or create a skit. To my happy surprise, Jack asked me to choreograph a dance for the evening's event.

I invited all the campers to create a dance with me. Seemingly all at once, thirty eager children told me they couldn't wait to participate. Remembering that "Twelfth Street Rag" was a popular song during that year, I decided to use it for the dance. It was a fast, catchy tune with an upbeat melody. I derived endless pleasure from the children's excitement, which was totally contagious. They could not wait to put the record on of the song to begin rehearsals, and we spent those last two weeks practicing the dance until we knew it from start to finish. It was a source of enjoyment and camaraderie for us all.

Our dance was the last piece on the night's program. I was so proud watching the children as they performed. They were having the time of their lives, smiling and winking at one another as they danced with assurance and joyful abandon.

When the performance was over, the children rightfully "brought down the house." There was silence for a moment. Then, the audience rose to their feet and applauded the dancers with gusto. Parents and friends alike could not only see but feel the same energy the children felt.

Our accomplishment was extremely gratifying. I knew this because each of the campers gave me the biggest hug when the event was over.

I knew Jack was delighted because he came to my bungalow just before we left to return home.

"Lois," he said, "you did a great job, and I am giving you a little extra money to emphasize my appreciation for taking over so well. Let's talk about next year. You have a job again if you like."

That summer in so many meaningful ways, was unforgettable, and prepared me for my future passion for dance.

9
MARTHA GRAHAM

"Great dancers are not great because of their technique; they are great because of their passion."
~Martha Graham

Loved, revered, respected, and admired are the qualities that can be attributed to the artistry of Martha Graham. For those in the dance world, Graham was regarded as an icon and a creative thinker. I consider myself fortunate to have been among her many students.

Martha Graham was unparalleled as a dancer and choreographer, and her luminous style is cause for both celebration and reflection. Her works were multifaceted, thoughtful and erudite. She created the world-renowned School of Contemporary Dance that emphasized excellence in creativity and optimal body development and that continues to this day.

Having known of Graham's reputation from childhood, I felt as though I were walking on hallowed ground when I first became a student at the school as a teenager. The discipline was unique, the technique inspiring and the dance dynamic.

After taking a class, it felt as though my body and soul were in perfect alignment.

Even as a child, I was drawn to dance for its discipline, its unbounded creative energy, and its uniqueness as an art form. I had the good fortune to be introduced to dance by my parents, who took me to many dance performances when I was growing up. Among those performances was one by the thrilling Graham company.

Dance is unlike any other art form in that the body is its instrument. Its qualities are a melding of the visual, physical, and spatial.

Except for the musical accompaniment, it is silent by its very nature; yet it communicates feelings, ideas, and thoughts loud enough that it resonates with the viewer and can sometimes turn out to be more articulate than the spoken word.

Graham powerfully expressed that idea in her essay, "I Am a Dancer." She wrote, "I hear the phrase the dance for life. It is an expression that touches me deeply, for the instrument through which the dance speaks is also the instrument by which all the primaries of life are made manifest. It holds in its memory all matters of life and death and love."

Graham founded her school in 1926 in a tiny Carnegie Hall studio. Although I was familiar with the Graham company, I discovered the Graham technique itself in the early 1950s as a freshman and a dance major at Adelphi College (now University). The difference between seeing a Graham performance and personally experiencing the technique is like the difference between night and day.

The hallmark of the Graham technique is the opposition of "contraction and release." In essence, it is a stylized representation of the human breathing cycle and human emotions. Graham's thought process in developing the technique was simple and logical, yet the resulting movements were humanely related, brilliant, and revolutionary.

As a woman, it is reasonable for me to mention Graham's reference to contractions. It is deeply a construct that is humanly meaningful with its allusion to the act of giving birth wherein emotions and a focused breathing cycle are heightened during the experience and the joy of releasing new life. More universally, Graham's technique taps into the human condition of tensing up during stressful times and the pleasurable release that "letting go" of that tension the body breathes such as a welcome sigh of relief.

For her students, a class taught by Graham offered both a distinct challenge and a huge reward. She did not hold back from correcting her pupils. There were those in my class who tried to shrink into the back of the classroom to remove themselves from being seen. I welcomed the corrections no matter how negative they might seem. I was there to learn and felt that being seen was in my best interest and especially so under Graham's tutelage.

Graham's artistry was innovative and exciting. Consequently, she attracted other gifted dancers and budding choreographers.

Her influential teaching inspired these dancers to create their own companies. In some respects, they incorporated her technique in creating their own genres. Noted names such as Pearl Lang, Alvin Ailey, Merce Cunningham, Paul Taylor, Lar Lubovitch, Jacqulyn Buglisi, and Pascal Rioult were students at the Graham school. They became members of the Graham Company and then created their own dance troupes.

In addition to my classes with her my personal reflections of Martha Graham are twofold:

The first involves a mistake I made when I was enrolled as a student at Martha's school. The rules were to wear a foot covering like ballet slippers while walking in the halls of the school's building. I was cognizant of the rule and always tried to follow it. The rule was a health-safety measure. The studio was in New York City and could be a haven for germs. While the classes were taught barefoot, wearing a foot covering in the halls was essential for keeping illness at bay.

On this one day, I had forgotten to bring my slippers and was unfortunately late.

Breathless, I ran into the school building, and up the stairs to change into my leotard and tights in the dressing room. Hurriedly, I dashed out of the dressing room and down the stairs in my bare feet where I was met by Martha Graham standing in front of me. I stopped immediately.

"Dear," she said, "where are your slippers?"

"I know, I know," I said, trying to catch my breath. "I was running late today and forgot to bring them."

"Next time," she quickly replied, in her famously formidable manner, "do not forget them," then turned on her heels and walked away.

The other instance of my interaction with Martha came about when David was the general counsel for the Avis-Rent-A-Car corporation.

One member of the Avis staff was a young woman assigned to the company's special projects division. The year was 1972, early in the summer. I was invited by the special projects person to attend a Halston fashion show. Halston was Graham's personal clothes designer, as well as the designer for some of her performance costumes. Avis hired Halston to design their service uniforms, which led to my invitation to the show.

My children had just left to attend summer sleep-away camp. I decided to take advantage of the time alone to sign-up for the daily classes at the Graham school and then go to the Halston fashion show.

I drove into the city, registered for the classes, and soon after arrived at Halston's studio.

As I sat down, I noticed an array of celebrities at the opposite side of the room. Wide-eyed, I saw Liza Minnelli sitting comfortably in one chair. Next to her was the popular comedienne, Phylis Diller. The ill-fated Steve Rubell was sitting next to Diller. I then spotted Gower Champion, the noted dancer and choreographer, and a wonder of wonders, sitting next to him was Martha Graham, herself elegantly dressed in Halston.

The models and the clothes worn were all beautiful, but my gaze was on Martha. I whispered to the special projects person that Martha was sitting directly across from us and that I had just come from her studio after registering for her summer classes.

The minute the fashion show ended, I jumped up from my chair and ran over to Martha. She greeted me with a smile. I explained two things to her as to my presence at the fashion show: the fact that my husband was the general counsel for Avis and that I'd been invited by the corporation's representative because Halston was recently hired as the designer of the Avis service uniforms, and I had just registered for the summer classes at her studio because my children were at a sleep-away camp.

I remember Liza Minnelli, Phyllis Diller, and Steve Rubell looking and listening intently as I related my story to Martha and to Gower Champion.

Martha paused, looked at Gower, then looked back at me. She raised her arms and clasped my face between both of her hands. "Gower," she said, "can you believe this child has children?"

I did not wash my face for a week.

More than fifty years have passed since that memorable day and my other unforgettable experiences with Martha Graham. The opportunity to have been associated with such a great artist and the life-affirming movement she brought into my world is something I will always remember.

10

A SPECIAL RELATIONSHIP

"Instead of saying a prayer, (Pearl Lang on religious dancing) they danced a prayer. That means you have your whole body dedicated to the moment, and there are many quotes from King David, 'All my bones utter thy praise. That's dancing for me.'
~ Pearl Lang

"A life being enacted onstage is a thing of utter fascination for me. And acting, it may begin out of vanity, but you hope that it is taken over by something else. I hope I've climbed over the vanity hurdle."
~ Joseph Wiseman

The extraordinary artistry and profound Judaic faith of two fellow New Yorkers were the foundation of what became a long-term, irreplaceably meaningful relationship in David's and my lives.

Pearl Lang and Joseph Wiseman were widely admired artists and Yiddishists who exemplified deep respect for their Jewish heritage both in their individual fields of artistry and in their loving relationship as husband and wife.

For more than five decades it was my good fortune to have been associated with Pearl, a noted dancer and prolific choreographer and her husband Joe, an acclaimed actor on both stage and screen.

Their work was something I admired for many years. Later, they became close personal friends.

Pearl would all but light up the stage as a dance soloist and member of the Martha Graham Dance Company and Joe would have his audience absorbed in his many distinguished theater and film performances.

The noted critic Deborah Jowitt wrote that Pearl was "one of the few dancers whom it is safe to call great." Regarding her dance compositions, a Le Figaro reviewer stated, "Her choreography illuminates the stage with its lyricism."

Joe was also renowned for his many roles. Among them were his performances as Dr. No, in the 1962 film of the same name and the unstable hood in the 1949 stage production of "Detective Story," and its follow-up 1951 film adaptation portrayals that were praised for their chilling realism.

Most notably, for his work on stage, Joe received the Drama Desk Award for his luminous depiction of J. Robert Oppenheimer in the 1969 Lincoln Center's production of "In the Matter of J. Robert Oppenheimer."

Pearl and Joe were devoted to their creative work and thrived both independently and jointly. You could not think of one without the other. It was always, "Pearl and Joe."

It was thrilling to watch them on stage reciting Yiddish poetry (with English translation), appearances that demonstrated their love and fluency in the language.

They were a beautiful couple as artists, in their demeanor and in their sensitivity to others. David and I were the fortunate beneficiaries of their wonderful kindness and friendship over the years.

My personal association with Pearl began when I first studied under her at the Martha Graham School of Contemporary Dance in the early 1950's. Her classes were energizing and inspiring, not only for the breadth of the movement she taught, but for the emphasis that she vibrantly expressed regarding her Jewish heritage. (That heritage became even more apparent after she established her own company in 1952, "The Pearl Lang Dance Theater." Of the sixty plus works she created for the company, more than half were based on Jewish culture).

It wasn't long before my association with Pearl expanded in numerous ways. For example, our daughter, Susie also studied at the Graham school with Pearl as her teacher. In addition, there were many times Susie and I took classes together as mother and daughter. Subsequently, I became a member of the staff of the dance company after Susie graduated from high school.

But best of all, Pearl and Joe came to be like family for David and me.

It was always a joy to include them in our Hanukkah and Passover celebrations.

In this, as in many other ways, the relationship between the four of us deepened: we considered ourselves to be colleagues, friends and members of each other's families.

I fondly recall many evenings David and I spent in Pearl and Joe's company. Our conversations were interesting, eclectic and fun.

Joe, Pearl, and the author's mother Dora Warshauer celebrating Passover.

Topics under discussion would include current events, dance and the theater to name but a few. Their interest in our family was touching, and they always asked, "So, what's new with your children?" I recall Pearl referring to Joe as "Jussel," which was her Hebrew and loving transliteration of his given name. And Joe or "Jussel," usually had a story or a joke to tell that together with the Jewish dialect he brandished to narrate the tale would have us doubled over in laughter.

Invariably, dance dominated our conversations. Pearl would forever be sharing her plans for choreographing a new piece including ideas for the music and dancers she envisioned to perform the work.

While all of Pearl's repertory was compelling in its scope of reference, the pieces centered on Judaica consistently had the greatest impact on her audiences. Among those pieces were "Shirah," which was based on a parable of Rabbi Nachman of Bratslav. "The Tailor's Megillah" which told the story of

Purim, and "The Possessed," *a work* based on S. Ansky's, "The Dybbuk."

Of all her Judaica works, however, the most emotionally powerful was "Commemoration to the Holocaust," which was first performed at the 92nd Street Y in 1977.

I saw the work in 1982, which was also performed at the 92nd Street Y.

I was eager to attend the performance, after reading about it previously. However, it was being rendered on an evening that David was working, and he would be unable to accompany me. He said, "You should go just the same," and added, "I know that I'll see it another time."

So, I drove into the city to the theater and bought a ticket.

The work consisted of individual sections, each one a heartfelt moving memorial to the victims of the Holocaust. In counterpoint, the opening piece excerpted from "The Possessed," expressed in Hasidic dance, the joys of life before the horrors of war.

Among the other works in "Commemoration" were: "A Seder Night," which recalled the ritual meal celebrated at Passover for the spirits of those who were no longer there, profoundly danced by Pearl. "I Never Saw Another Butterfly," based on poems written by the children imprisoned by the Nazis in the Terezin concentration camp from 1942 to 1944; and "Kaddish," whose riveting choreography captured the essence of Pearl's passion and compassion for each and every Jew, if not for all humanity.

I could not move when the performance ended. I felt glued to my seat. Somehow, I managed to get up and walk out of the theater and back to my car.

A SPECIAL RELATIONSHIP 51

Upon my return home, David seemed to sense my still dazed expression. He asked, "Good performance?"

"Absolutely astonishing," I replied.

By now, my mind was racing. My children were getting older, and I could begin to think about finding a job. I had been considering connecting myself to a dance company and working as an administrator. It was at this moment; I had the realization that the time and place were now.

I decided to call Pearl's office the next day.

When we spoke, I told Pearl, who I barely knew at the time, that David and I greatly admired her work as a dancer and choreographer and wondered whether she would consider hiring me as one of her administrative assistants.

I vividly recall a long pause on the phone, until Pearl said, "I desperately need an administrative assistant, Lois but I wouldn't have any money to pay you," but not before adding in the same breath, "let me think about it." We ended the conversation on that tentative note.

The phone rang several weeks later. It was Pearl. She explained, "I just received a small grant that includes the salary for an assistant. Does that interest you?"

I responded instantly, "Yes, thank you, it does."

That phone call led to my many decades relationship with Pearl as a colleague, friend and adopted family member.

It was also during those years that David's and my connection with both Pearl and Joe became meaningfully close.

On many occasions, Joe would call me concerned about Pearl. "She is in her seventies and still dancing," he would say, "Enough!" His insistent but caring objections were non-stop but not out of place. "And all those hours of rehearsals, I worry about her health."

I tried to assure him that although Pearl puts in many hours, she took care of herself, and that for her, age was just a number. I also reminded him of how her love of dance served to energize her. Around that time, as if to prove my point, I referred Joe to Pearl's performance when she was seventy-seven and just after a hip replacement. Her mobility was that of a woman twenty years her junior.

My responsibilities as a member of Pearl's administrative staff included such tasks as scheduling rehearsals, keeping track of the company's finances and working as a fundraiser.

Much was going on in Pearl's life during this period. For example, after more than a decade "The Possessed" was finally close to being recreated cinematically. Only ten thousand dollars was needed to complete the film. I had a thought. *Why not apply to the Steven Spielberg Righteous Persons Foundation?*

I ran the suggestion by Pearl, who considered it for a moment and then said, "Great idea. But do you think we have a chance to get it?"

There was no question in my mind, and I said so. "We have nothing to lose and besides it's a remarkable piece." We agreed that I would write a letter to the foundation and include all of the reviews of the work and then follow-through with a phone call to give our request a personal touch.

The letter explained that I knew the foundation must receive many requests, but that "The Possessed" was unique not only for its exceptional choreography but as a literary, historical, and artistic achievement for now and for posterity.

Several months passed.

The phone rang early one morning.

"Lois, we got it! Ten-thousand dollars!" It was Pearl, breathlessly sharing the exciting news. "No, I take that back. You got it. Thank you! Thank you!"

It was extremely gratifying to see the film screened at Lincoln Center and a thrill that Lois and David Schaffer and the Steven Spielberg Righteous Persons Foundation were listed in the credits.

During my tenure working with Pearl, she called me one Sunday morning to ask a favor. She told me that someone she knew was flying to Israel that night and was going to be seeing the philanthropist Bethsabee de Rothschild. As Pearl had continually been giving thought to finding outside sources of support for her company, she believed this was as opportune a time as any to approach a potential donor, even if through a third party.

Her request was for me to assemble all of her company's literature together with a letter asking for funding. Pearl said she and Joe would drive out from the city to my home on Long Island to pick everything up later that day.

Several hours after that the doorbell rang. It was Pearl and Joe standing at my front door with a huge bouquet of flowers.

On many occasions I would drive into the city to pick Pearl and Joe up to attend some event and then drive them back to their apartment.

As I drove off, Joe would say, "Call me when you get home."

My reply was always, "I'm fine. It's not necessary."

In his most booming voice, he would repeat emphatically, "You will call me when you get home," then pause to say, "or else I won't sleep a wink."

Invariably, upon my return home, David was on the phone with Joe. "Yes, Joe, she just walked in safe and sound. Thank you for calling."

As I look around my home, I see many reminders of Pearl and Joe in the gifts they so graciously gave us. There is a glass bowl we received as a house present for Passover that I use every year on that holiday. There is a hamsa that is displayed on a wall in our family room. Then there is a copy of Ben Shahn's book, "Ecclesiastes," a gift for a wedding anniversary. David and I cherish all of these mementos because they are tangible representations that speak to a warm, multifaceted friendship.

Pearl and Joe died in 2009 within months of each other. Pearl succumbed to a heart attack in February following a second surgical procedure and Joe died in October. Independently and together, their lives were a legacy of artistry and Judaic heritage for future generations.

David and I will forever be grateful for the special relationship we had with Pearl and Joe, two extraordinary people who enriched our lives spiritually, artistically and personally, providing us with joyful reflections that continue to this day.

11

UNORTHODOX PAIRINGS

"Culture is the arts elevated to a set of beliefs."
~ *Thomas Wolfe*

It is fascinating to think how things that were once considered to be unacceptable are now a normal occurrence.

For example, wine pairings. Not all that long ago, it was thought that when eating fish, it was only acceptable to drink white wine. The opposite held true regarding meat: red wine was the only accepted accompaniment.

Dress codes have also changed, especially in the workplace. Suits and ties for men and skirts and blouses for women were the dress conventions that had to be adhered to.

And while it is not my choice, tattoos and body piercings, which were once associated with rebellion, are now mainstream and widely accepted as self-expression.

This same mainstreaming holds true in the world of dance. There were the genres of classical ballet and modern dance, for which it was once thought, "never the twain shall meet."

What are the differences between ballet and modern dance? Broadly speaking, they utilize different energies. In classical ballet, the movements are technically exact, emphasizing balance, strength and flexibility. In modern dance, balance, strength and flexibility are also evident but with fewer constraints. Another difference is that in classical ballet, women wear toe shoes while barefoot is the norm in modern dance.

Ballet's beginnings date to the Renaissance courts of Italy in the 15th century, having been adopted from an earlier French art form that embraced a highly structured vocabulary.

Modern dance began in the late 19th and early 20th centuries and was a "freer" form of expression that broke away from ballet's structured movements.

Isadora Duncan, the acclaimed modernist, was known as the first proponent of this philosophy and movement style.

Even as modern dance was arriving on the scene, Russian ballet also was becoming prominent in the late 19th and early 20th centuries. Known for its rigorous technique, it placed emphasis on precision in capturing the interest of the international dance community.

In the late '70s and early '80s, two celebrated Russian ballet dancers, Mikhail Baryshnikov and Rudolph Nureyev, were invited as guest performers at major American modern dance organizations, among them were the Martha Graham and Paul Taylor dance companies. The brilliant Baryshnikov caused a sensation as the principal dancer with the Martha Graham Dance Company, starting with his inaugural performance in 1987.

Rudolph Nureyev was invited as a guest artist with the Murray Louis Dance Company in 1978. What follows is the story of a serendipitous surprise of events that led me to be in the audience witnessing a thrilling dance performance and subsequently meeting one of the world's most renowned ballet artists.

Murray Louis (1926-2016) was born Murray Louis Fuchs in Brooklyn, New York. He was the co-founder of the Nikolais/Louis Foundation of Dance and was the collaborator and companion of Alwin Nikolais (who was respectfully referred to as "Nik") for over forty years.

Louis studied with major modern choreographers Anna Halprin and Hanya Holm. It was while studying at Colorado College with Holm in the late '40s that Louis met Alwin Nikolais. Their subsequent collaboration included dance productions at the Henry Street Settlement Playhouse where Nikolais led the dance program.

In 1953, Louis formed his own dance company. Prior to merging their separate companies in 1989, Louis and Nikolais were the subjects of the 1987 PBS American Masters documentary, *Alwin Nikolais and Murray Louis: Nik and Murray*.

In addition to his work in dance, Louis was an accomplished author, publishing two collections of essays, *Inside Dance* (1980) and *On Dance* (1992). He also staged works for various dance companies including the Royal Danish Ballet, the Hamburg Ballet, the Scottish Ballet and the Batsheva and Limon dance companies. He was awarded two Guggenheim fellowships, and grants from the Rockefeller, Mellon and Ford foundations. Moreover, he was also a recipient of the Dance Magazine Award and was named a Knight of the Order of Arts and Letters by the French government.

Together with Nikolais, he choreographed and staged the musical, *Lenny and the Heartbreakers,* for Joseph Papp's New York Shakespeare Festival.

My association with Murray Louis began as a student at his Nikolais and Louis dance studio in Manhattan in the 1970s.

A conversation with Louis was thoughtful and poignant. He had an uncommon insight into the beauty and theory of dance. I found myself constantly mesmerized by his incisive views about life and dance, which included a desire to meld modern dance and classic overtones to create a new model for movement.

It was due to a combined commission that Louis received from the 16th International Festival of Dance at the Theatre Champs-Elysees in Paris, the Taormina Art Festival in Sicily and the American Dance Festival that he was given the chance to collaborate with Nureyev.

Thanks to our many conversations, Louis knew of the pleasure I derived from hosting receptions at our home and my deep-felt commitment to dance. I was ecstatic when he told me that the great dancer Rudolph Nureyev had been invited to be a guest artist with his dance company in a performance at the Minskoff Theater in New York City. As if that weren't enough, Louis asked me to coordinate a reception for Nureyev at the Waldorf Astoria following the performance earlier that night.

The idea that the international star, Rudolph Nureyev, would be performing in New York, and that I was asked to coordinate this extraordinary event in his honor, was almost beyond my imagination. Not only that, I would also have the opportunity to actually meet this legendary dancer.

I couldn't help but remember the sensation he caused as the first Russian dancer to defect from the Soviet Union. He was a soloist with the Leningrad (St. Petersburg) Kirov Ballet Company, now known as the Mariinsky. In June 1961, having performed in France with Kirov, Nureyev was at Le Bourget airport in Paris, where, evading Soviet security, he requested asylum in the West.

One can only picture the display in the airport of Nureyev's historic, steadfast bravery to escape the confines of the KGB and USSR. He not only set himself free from the constraints of Russian governmental control but also paved the way for later Russian dancers' defections, including Baryshnikov's.

The schedule for the Nureyev evening was shared with me by Louis's assistants. It was to include a cocktail reception and dinner in a private suite at the Waldorf.

I was given *carte blanche* to organize a menu for the reception and dinner and put in touch with a caterer. I remember sharing the elation I felt with David regarding the event and my own little contribution. We were both thrilled about being at the reception and about attending Nureyev's performance.

Louis had choreographed a solo work for Nureyev. On stage, the great dancer was larger than life. His performance was compelling, strong and streamlined. It was a moment that made my spirit soar as I witnessed the pairing of a world-renowned classical Russian ballet dancer with modes of modern dance that was nothing less than electrifying.

When the performance concluded, David and I scurried over to the suite allotted to me at the Waldorf for the reception.

It was exhilarating to think that at last I would meet Nureyev.

Upon arriving at the suite, David and I marveled at the exquisitely organized table of food and floral arrangements. The aura of joy was unmistakable.

Servers were standing at the buffet table filling plates of food for those who had arrived early including a few of Louis' dancers and others who were major donors to his dance company.

Soon other guests began arriving in droves. I kept looking at the doorway expecting to see the man of the hour. But no Nureyev. It seemed endless, waiting for him to make his appearance.

Finally, there he was. Exhibiting a pale complexion and dressed in a belted beige raincoat and cap, he was shorter than he appeared on stage. I ran up to him and said, "Welcome." He paused for a moment and replied, "Wodka!" Not even a "thank you." Just "wodka!" I knew he must have been "thirsty" from all the energy he'd expended on stage, but my first feeling of this dismissal was one of disappointment.

As the evening progressed, guests and dancers milled about, and lively conversation prevailed. I watched Louis as he squired Nureyev around the room, introducing him to important members of his company and donor group. It was an honor for David and me when Louis eventually introduced us to Nureyev and mentioned that I was responsible for coordinating the reception. Nureyev kindly shook my hand as his acknowledgment of understanding. And that was that.

Too soon it seemed, the gathering drew to a close, and all of the guests began their departure including Nureyev.

I noticed Louis and Nureyev giving each other a warm hug.

Other than Nureyev's passionate performance on stage, this was the only time that he showed any emotion.

Upon reflection, Nureyev's and Louis' inspired collaboration at the Minskoff demonstrated how this seminal meeting of two artists whose pairing might have appeared unorthodox was proven to be beautifully valid.

12

DANCING FOR LIFE

"Believe you can, and you are halfway there."
~ *Theodore Roosevelt.*

It was in late spring of 1987 that an article in the New York Times caught my eye.

The article announced the formation of an event called Dancing for Life. It was slated to be a gala benefit with ticket prices ranging from $50 to $5,000 and scheduled to be held at Lincoln Center's New Yor State Theater (now the Koch Theater) in early October of that year.

The funds raised would be donated in multiple ways: in support of AIDS research, AIDS related education and for AIDS care in the United States. The benefit's goal for funds to be raised was set at $1.4 million.

The catastrophic AIDS epidemic had been widely covered in the media in the early '80's. At that time, the as-yet-unidentified disease was killing off a specific group of people, mainly gay men, many of whom were engaged in the arts such as fashion, theater and dance.

In 1985 two notable plays were produced on the New York stage. Both plays were written by authors who were affected by the disease. The first of the plays, *The Normal Heart* was written by Larry Kramer and the other, *As Is,* was written by William Hoffman. Both plays forcefully brought issues of health, sexuality and mortality to the public's attention.

Lar Lubovitch - Courtesy of the Lubovitch Dance Company: Headshot used for the Martha Hill Dance Fund.

Creative works such as these were a clear and vital response to the epidemic and helped to raise awareness and challenge widespread misconceptions about AIDS and its underlying virus, HIV.

Dancing for Life was the first organized event to publicly and artistically embrace the need to focus on the epidemic that was taking the lives of so many talented dancers and choreographers.

The idea for the event was proposed three years prior to its production by the much-admired modern dancer and choreographer, Lar Lubovitch, someone who was deeply saddened by the deaths of people in the world of dance in New York and elsewhere. The intensity of Lubovitch's feelings inspired him to use the power of dance to address this issue by and for the dance community. Acting on his idea, he gathered a steering committee together.

The iconic choreographer, Jerome Robbins, was named the event's artistic director.

Some time later there was a call for volunteers in a New York Times article covering this event. Volunteers were needed to help with the day-to-day production of the benefit by carrying out such tasks as addressing and stamping the envelopes for the printed invitations and answering phones calls.

The request to become a volunteer intrigued me, given my love of dance and the critically important cause for which the benefit was being held. Consequently, I found myself driving daily into Manhattan during that summer and fall, to the event's production office near Lincoln Center. My decision to become involved defined a sense of purpose and fulfillment deep within me.

The plans for the event were exciting and huge. Thirteen of New York's major dance companies, from ballet to modern, were scheduled to perform.

The participating companies were the Alvin Ailey American Dance Theater, American Ballet Theater, the Merce Cunningham Dance Theater, Dance Theater of Harlem, Laura Dean Dancers and Musicians, the Feld Ballet, the Martha Graham Dance Company, the Joffrey Ballet, the Paul Taylor Dance Company, the Mark Morris Dance Group, the New York City Ballet, Twyla Tharp Dance and the Lar Lubovitch Dance Company.

All the people in the production office, which included a total of four other volunteers, were warm, welcoming and committed to making the event a success in terms of its artistic achievements and as "a call to arms" to fighting the disease.

Although my writing hand was sore by the end of each day, the hours spent at the office were fun and productive and by any measure worth the extremely minor discomfort.

One day, I took a phone call. A voice on the other end sounded foreign. "This is Mischa." I did a double take. He continued, "I want four tickets."

In disbelief, I realized I was listening to the voice of none other than the world-renowned dancer, Mikhail Baryshnikov!

I managed to collect myself and sheepishly answered, "yes, of course," and duly hung up the phone, I was still astonished at the conversation I had just had.

Approximately two weeks before the event all of the volunteers were offered two $500 tickets for the price of one.

David and I were thrilled to have the opportunity to see such an incredible array of artists performing in one place and in support of such an important cause.

I recall our bittersweet conversation as we were preparing to drive into Manhattan for the gala evening. We shared our despair about the dancers who had succumbed to the disease but our gratitude that we were able to participate with efforts to help towards a cure both personally and financially. And we shared our admiration for Lar Lubovitch. It was his forethought that the event was created in the first place

We immediately felt the electricity, energy and spirit that prevailed as we entered the theater. Prominent people from all walks of life were present: businessmen and women, and politicians as well as those associated with the arts.

I remember being shown to our seats and reading the program notes while eagerly anticipating the start of the evening's performances.

The reality outweighed my anticipation.

The lights dimmed, and a thunderous applause erupted as Mikhail Baryshnikov entered the stage. He spoke for several minutes. The message he delivered was that this was a war on AIDS but emphatically he believed that humanity "will win."

It was inspiring to listen to Baryshnikov's remarks. Graciously, he thanked all of those who donated their time and efforts to the event. He made a special acknowledgment of Jerome Robbins as the event's artistic director and announced with great appreciation that the $1.4 million fundraising goal had been reached.

Energy and spirit continued throughout the evening as each of the companies performed their work.

Lar Lubovitch - Courtesy of the Lubovitch Dance Company
(Photo by Rose Eichenbaum from Masters of Movement.)

While all of the pieces were memorable, Lubovitch's duet, *Concerto Six-Twenty-Two,* garnered the most rapturous applause and rightly so, with its vibrant display of human emotion.

The distinguished scholar and author, Warren Bennis, said, "Leadership is the capacity to translate vision into reality" Lar Lubovitch's vision and his efforts on behalf of Dancing for Life were the very embodiment of the creative leadership of which Bennis spoke. After all these years, my participation continues to have an impact on my life and gives me hope that a cure for AIDS may one day be found.

13

SUSIE

"Singularly blessed"
~Joan Didion

Buried deep within my psyche are reflections regarding Susie and the connection we had as mother and daughter in the world of dance.

In December 2008, Susie's life was tragically cut short by a teenaged burglar in possession of a stolen handgun.

Among her many attributes, Susie was movement oriented. She was a swimmer, a runner and later a physical fitness instructor. It was due to those activities, along with my own training in dance, mobility literally became a way of life for her physically and spiritually.

It was thrilling to take classes with Susie at the Martha Graham School of Contemporary Dance. Afterward, the classes' pleasures were augmented by discussions we would have during our trips home.

Our classes at the school would begin with floor exercises. During that portion of the class, I used to watch Susie stretching, as she elongated her legs into second position, easily putting her torso down flat onto the floor. It was a marvel to see my daughter, already nimble and strong at age fifteen, in what seemed to be an effortless execution of this position. She was practically a human stretch band.

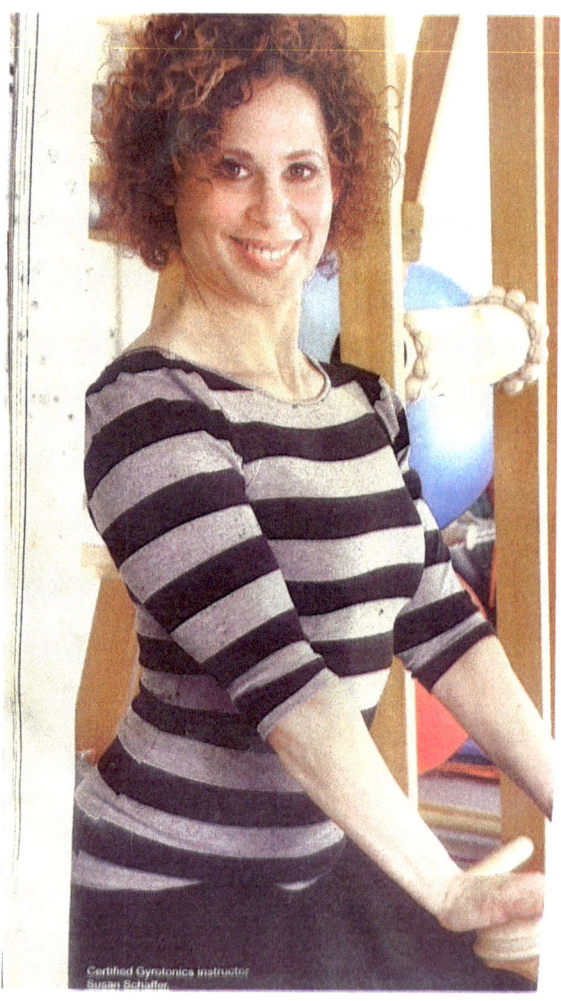

Certified Gyrotonics instructor Susan Schaffer

Our mother-daughter connection to dance included attending dance concerts together. This was a wonderful source of enjoyment for us, comparing the various companies and our thoughts about their performance and choreography.

Susie was inspired by movement and worked hard to become certified in Pilates and Gyrotonic.

Just one year prior to her death, she had realized her dream of opening her own Pilates and Gyrotonic studio in St. Louis as a certified instructor in both techniques.

Susie was greatly admired for her talent and created a large following during the brief time she had teaching in her studio. A television newscaster in St. Louis heard about Susie's classes and interviewed her. The newscaster subsequently became one of Susie's clients.

After Susie's death, David and I were invited to a performance under the auspices of the non-profit Dance St. Louis organization that featured the Pilobolus Dance Company. The evening centered around a tribute to Susie and the devotion she lavished on her students, her work and all that she accomplished within her short career. It was a bittersweet evening and attended by many of Susie's students.

Each one of those students made it a point to share their heartfelt sentiments with us regarding the impact Susie had on their lives. Their tributes were eloquent, both personally and professionally.

Once you met Susie you were enveloped in her boundless, kindhearted energy as a human being, a dancer and as an esteemed instructor in special movement styles.

"Movement comes from within" and "feel as though you are pushing the walls out" initiates two mental images that resonate with me. Those images were beautifully expressed by various dance teachers I've met over the years that can be translated to Susie's personality.

The first image emanates from the idea that movement comes from within. In that regard, Susie was inspired by activities----dance and movement---that manifested themselves in her career choice and the physical means to share that choice with others. To describe that idea more plainly, an arm or a leg does not move by itself---it's what is inside the heart and soul that moves those limbs. Susie's affection for people was shown by the way she so gently guided others in her classes in accordance with this idea.

The second image comes from the notion of pushing the walls out. This image owes to the idea that in dance it is possible to feel the sense of one's own expansiveness, to push out beyond oneself. In a way, Susie "pushed out" her horizons in movement including her commitment to swimming and running, to dance and finally, Pilates and Gyrotonic, not only for her own benefit but for that of others as well.

It is a wondrous dichotomy as I reflect both on my life with Susie regarding dance and simultaneously on the future. As I did with Susie, I revel in the fact that her children inherited their mother's love of an art form that encompasses physical prowess and emotional connection. Even more meaningful, and future thinking, is that Susie lives in their energy and potentially in the vitality and promise of her grandchildren.

14

EXERCISE: ITS UPS AND DOWNS

"If you do not expect the unexpected you will not find it, for it is not to be reached by search or trail."
~ Heraclitus

The years seem to fly by. It is almost unbelievable that I am an octogenarian but more like closer to my 90th year. Yet, I am grateful that I am more mobile than most people my age. As a former student at Martha Graham's School of Contemporary Dance, I remember well how mobility and flexibility were all but a precondition of accomplishment in dance and the extent to which I was fortunate to develop those attributes.

Studying at the Graham school was a joyous experience. Those classes taught by Martha Graham and Pearl Lang contributed to my sense of self and well-being in addition to my love of the art form.

The ability to be mobile and feel your body stretch to increase its flexibility can be most gratifying, pushing beyond yourself, feeling your own expansiveness, making a connection between your mind, body and soul and increasing your strength and mobility.

Though I no longer take dance classes, remaining physically active and mobile is still important to me for my health and happiness.

Consequently, I have become a walker. I was a runner for thirty years; however, in my late eighties, I am no longer able to continue at the pace I was accustomed to at a younger age.

So, whenever possible, I will venture out for my physical well being, a venture often, of late, not without its mishaps. The following stories, as you will see, might have made me or anyone else for that matter, wonder if my outdoor physical activity was worth it.

I was scheduled to attend an early evening meeting during the summer of 2024 a couple of miles from my home in Great Neck.

There was a cool summer breeze, ideal weather to get in some cardio activity.

So, I decided to take a brisk walk to the meeting. Happily, I was both enjoying the outdoors and fulfilling my goal of getting to the meeting.

As I was walking, I tripped on a piece of wire stretched unseen across the sidewalk causing me to take a flying leap that resulted in a fall landing me on my lip.

It was bloody. All I could think of was thank G-d. I didn't hit my head or lose any teeth. Just a bloody lip.

A kind gentleman driving his car stopped after seeing me take that tumble. He gave me his handkerchief and offered to drive me wherever I needed to go.

I knew I must have looked terrible, but I was still mobile. I thanked the Good Samaritan profusely and said I was fine. My wish was to continue walking.

I arrived at my meeting with people looking at me aghast, asking what had happened. "Just a fat, bloody lip from a fall," I told them.

One of the people at the meeting, trying to be kind said, "Lois, you walk too fast."

Trying to be kind in turn, I said, "I'm so glad I can still walk briskly. However, if it makes you feel better, I don't run anymore."

As with running, the desire to continue to walk for exercise comes from within my mind and body. In a sense, I am pushing beyond what I think I can normally do in order to maintain a feeling of strength and mobility, particularly outdoors. It is invigorating and has countless health benefits. So, I grab every chance I get to remain active in that manner.

During one late spring weekend in May 2024, David and I were visiting our grandchildren and great grandchild who live in St. Louis, reserving a room in a comfortable hotel near their home.

It was a Saturday afternoon, David was working on his laptop, our grandchildren were busy with their normal routines, and I had some free time before we would all get together later that day and into the evening for dinner.

It was the perfect opportunity to get some exercise. A purposeful walk was the answer, and the lack of humidity was conducive to accomplishing that goal.

Olive Boulevard is one of the main streets in suburban St. Louis County. It is a big, wide, busy thoroughfare and a street I have walked many times in the past.

I quickly changed into my running tights, shirt and sneakers and went outside. It was satisfying to feel the fresh air and soak up the pleasure of doing what I like to do, physical activity.

Almost immediately, I noticed cicadas flying all around me and on the ground. They were out in force. I exerted every effort to avoid their loud, unrelenting prevalence. I thought that I would stop walking several times and return to the hotel because their presence was, at the very least, unappealing. But needing the exercise, I continued walking for a few miles before returning to the hotel.

I was only a few blocks from my destination when out of nowhere a police car stopped in front of me while I was waiting for the light to change at a crosswalk.

A policeman, who looked all of fourteen, emerged from the car.

"Where are you going? What are you doing?" he asked.

I was a little surprised. But I answered him, even as I was in near disbelief that I was being stopped and questioned in the first place. "I'm out for my walk," I said.

"Where are you going?" he repeated.

"Back to my hotel, which is only a few blocks away."

He paused for a moment, then said, "Let me give you a ride."

"No, thank you. I am out for some exercise and don't want a ride."

It was obvious he was being as polite as possible and visibly concerned, but there was a steady stream of questions.

"Where are you from?" he inquired.

"New York."

"Yeah," he answered, "I can hear the accent. What are you doing here?"

"My husband and I are visiting our grandchildren."

Again, he said, "Let me give you a ride."

Also again, my answer was the same. "Thank you, but no, thank you."

By then I was getting the picture. This policeman, who barely looked out of puberty, saw what he thought was a little old lady with salt and pepper hair, walking alone on the street. She must have dementia.

The policeman did not change his tune. "You were walking in traffic."

"I don't know what you mean, but yes, I was walking on the sidewalk and stopping at crosswalks until the light turned green."

"Do you have an ID on you?"

"No," I answered. "Just my phone. Why would I need an ID if all I'm doing is walking?"

The fourteen-year-old repeated himself. "Let me give you a ride back to your hotel."

"I really appreciate your concern," I said. "However, I'm fine and want to complete my walk."

All the while we were talking, we were being bombarded by cicadas.

At that moment, unexpectedly, my cell-phone rang. It was my friend Barbara who lives in New York.

"Hi Barbara," I said.

"How are you? Where are you?" she asked. "I called your house-phone and got the answering machine. I thought I'd try you on your cell."

"Actually, we're in St. Louis, and I was out for a walk and am now talking to this nice policeman who is concerned for my "safety."

What I was thinking and what I said were two different things. In reality, I believed the policeman was verifying my sanity.

But I played it cool.

The policeman chimed in, "Let me talk to your friend."

I was a little taken aback but responded, "Absolutely why not. This is my friend Barbara. We've been friends for over 70 years, from high school and college."

I handed the phone to the policeman, who verified my mental state with Barbara and upon finishing his inquisition handed the phone back to me.

He still didn't give up.

Having mentioned my grandchildren, he asked, "Where do your grandchildren live?" I gave him the general information as to where they lived.

"I want to talk to them."

"That's silly. Besides, they're both at work."

He stopped questioning me for a moment.

"Look," I added, "I'm fine, but if you would like to allay your fears regarding my safety, I will call my husband who is also working and at our hotel."

"Sure," he said. "What does he do?"

"He's an attorney."

I dialed David's phone. When he answered, I said, "Hi'ya, hon. I'm on my way back to the hotel. You won't believe this, but I've been stopped by a policeman who is concerned about me. He would like to talk to you."

I handed the phone to the policeman, and he had a short conversation with David, who assured him that I was fine and just out for some exercise.

The policeman handed the phone back to me, finally persuaded that I was all right.

He began to get into his car but turned around and said, "Take a look at my back. Do you see any cicadas there?"

I looked and said, "Not one."

He drove off, and I finished walking back to the hotel to meet up with David.

We both laughed as we greeted each other in lighthearted relief.

During dinner that night, I shared the story of my encounter with my grandchildren and great grandchild. It was a tale that sent them all into gales of laughter.

One month later, we flew back to St. Louis to spend another weekend with family to celebrate our great grandchild's ninth birthday.

There was a quiet period, so I decided to go out for a walk. Thankfully, the cicadas were not around.

Before I went outside, David said, "Take care—and this time, try not to fall or get arrested."

COINCIDENCE OR UNKNOWN FORCE?

"Coincidence is God's way of remaining anonymous."
~ *Albert Einstein*

As uncanny as the phenomena might seem, connections, coincidences and reflections are intertwined and have continually resonated with me.

After Susie's death in December, 2008, those "phenomena" became even more important and meaningful, and I have found that sharing stories about Susie is cathartic and a means to keep her alive.

Susie's death was traumatic. While I would never negate the loss of anyone, it is much more devastating when it is the loss of a child. Her death was sudden and senseless. She was a single working mother of three young children and a victim of gun violence.

I have been a lifelong gun safety advocate. The shock of this tragedy was and still is unfathomable as I continue to feel its effects more than seventeen years later.

To keep Susie alive, I cling to any and all connections to her, the things she did, the foods and music she liked, the friends she had who became my friends. Acknowledging and welcoming these connections is a constant comfort, even to laugh about her "quirks."

Since Susie's death, random connections, or maybe many such coincidences have occurred. They include the following two incidents that have heightened my perception that Susie is guiding me beyond my understanding.

Many have considered the idea of the interconnectedness of human life, among them, Martin Luther King, Jr. and the Dalai Lama.

Martin Luther King, Jr. put it this way; "It really boils down to this: that life is interrelated. We are in an inescapable network of mutuality, tied into a single garment of destiny. Whatever affects one destiny, affects all indirectly."

The Dalai Lama said, "Our ancient experience confirms at every point that everything is linked together. Everything is inseparable."

The two instances described below made me think that an "unknown force" might be at work to maintain my connection to my daughter and in the process to help me nourish my truth as a mother.

The first grew out of the Sandy Hook Elementary School massacre in Newtown Connecticut early one Friday morning in December 2012. The devastation occurred exactly four years to the week after Susie was shot.

The media was flooded with the news on that Friday morning. Among those interviewed on television was Rabbi Shaul Praver, a first responder and the rabbi for the Pozner family, whose son,

Noah was one of the children who were slaughtered. Like the rest of the world, I watched in horror the ensuing reports detailing the unthinkable loss of twenty children and six adults.

Rabbi Praver was continually interviewed, and it was hard not to be moved by his wisdom, compassion and insights.

I called the rabbi's synagogue the following Monday morning to offer any help as a mother and a survivor. I spoke to the rabbi's assistant who introduced herself as "Susan." Together with the nearly overlapping dates, gave me pause to think, was this a coincidence?

I explained the reason for my call to Susan and my wish to speak to the rabbi, although I knew he was preoccupied.

Susan took my name and contact information. "The rabbi will call you," she said.

The following day I learned that Rabbi Praver grew up in Great Neck, where our family has lived for many years. He graduated from the same high school and was in the same class as Susie. More wonderment for me to ponder.

Rather than wait to hear from him, I immediately called Rabbi Praver again. Surprisingly, he answered the phone. I said, "My name is Lois Schaffer."

"I know who you are," he said and added, "I've said many prayers for Susie."

In September 2015, the young, brilliant attorney, Carey Gabay, who was Governor Andrew Cuomo's legal assistant was fatally shot during the J' Oeuvert Caribbean celebration in Brooklyn.

After reading about the shooting. I tried to connect with the family but was unsuccessful.

I learned that although Carey Gabay came from a disadvantaged circumstance, he studied, worked hard and was accepted at Harvard and Harvard Law School before becoming Governor Cuomo's legal assistant.

The following May I participated in the annual Mom's Demand Action march over the Brooklyn Bridge as a protest against gun violence and a plea for gun safety measures. Every year thousands of people attend the march. The event is composed of survivors of gun violence and others who are not. The camaraderie that prevails often leads to new friendships.

I happened to be walking next to a young woman. During the course of our conversation, I learned her name was Trenelle Gabay, Carey Gabay's widow.

So, what to make of these two unlikely occurrences?

Were they coincidences? Or was there some "unknown force"--- a guiding spirit---at work?

That is for you, dear reader, to decide.

One thing I do know is that these connections, whether they were coincidences or something deeper, have enriched my life and for that I am profoundly grateful.

16

ELLIOT FINEMAN

"There may be times when we are powerless to prevent injustice, but there must never be a time when we fail to protest."
Elie Wiesel

When I think about Elliot Fineman, I immediately think of passion and compassion, coupled with brilliance, creativity, activism, and a forceful quest for justice. After meeting Elliot, it was clear he was a "doer," an individual who would "jump right in" as a problem solver.

Elliot successfully served as an advisor for twenty-five years to prestigious Fortune 500 consulting firms such as Accenture, KPMG and Boston Consulting Group.

I was introduced to Elliot by Shaul Praver who was the Rabbi at Newtown, Connecticut. Our collective connection stemmed from similar unspeakable circumstances: the rabbi's losses at Sandy Hook Elementary School and the loss of Elliot's son, Michael, and my daughter, Susie, due to gun violence.

Michael was a forty-four-year-old father of three and a medic in the U.S. Special Forces. His murderer was a schizophrenic who had legally obtained a gun despite having been twice institutionalized for mental illness.

Both deaths had been sudden and violent. Susie was shot during a burglary in her home, and Michael's death occurred while he was at a restaurant with his wife and friends.

Typical of Elliot's nature, he did not waste a moment. Without hesitation, he closed his consulting firm and began his highly focused foray for justice in the death of his beloved son.

He became a strong, leading voice for a network of gun-violence victims and survivors including me and my family seeking to change America's gun laws. He was outspoken, with an energy to be reckoned with, exemplified by his radio and television appearances in addition to the many opinion articles that were published in newspapers such as the *Philadelphia Inquirer*.

Elliot's ability to engage people was quickly noted and led to appearances on CNBC, CNN, BBC, PBS, Australian television and China Central Television.

Elliot also hosted his own radio show, "It's the Guns, Stupid!" that included both nationally known guests as well as average American citizens who had been sadly drawn into the gun-violence issue. Concurrently, he founded the non-profit organization National Gun Victims Action Council (NGVAC).

It was in 2014 that Rabbi Praver connected me to Elliot.

Elliot was living in Chicago at that time; we communicated by email and arranged an initial phone call.

I will never forget that conversation. We laughed and cried, sharing our thoughts about the love of our families.

Sweetly, he asked, "Do you have a husband?"

"Yes, I do."

In my mind, his thoughtful, caring nature was quickly felt with the bevy of questions he asked me.

"How is your husband? What's his name? Is he working? What's his profession, and how is your relationship after your loss? I ask that question because I know of other marriages that have broken up due to the devastation."

First, I thanked Elliot for his compassion and concern and then responded to his questions.

"His name is David. He's an attorney and still in practice. And I know what you mean regarding broken marriages after the loss of a child. But to answer your question, he is the best human being ever, and truth be told, I think we became closer after Susie's death."

Elliot shared the fact that it was his good fortune to have two loves of his life. The first was his wife, Patricia, who died when she was only 44 years old. The second was Nancy, a lifelong companion who also passed away at a very young age.

"However," Elliot added, "my daughter Elissa possesses the strength and kindness of both those women."

Elissa lives in Atlanta. Elliot shared Elissa's caring nature with me when the COVID pandemic became so threatening. Elliot told me that she firmly stated, "You have no choice. I want you here with me so I can take care of you." So, Elliot moved from Chicago to Atlanta to live near Elissa.

Our telephone conversation was the beginning of a most meaningful friendship. We frequently discussed potential changes to gun-possession regulations to prevent tragedies like ours.

We both concurred that we would fight for those changes and remain undeterred by our grievous losses.

Elliot's words, "Lois, it's an epidemic," still resonate with me as he continued to fight in every way possible to stop these senseless killings.

My association with Elliot continued over a period of ten years. His story was told in my book, *From Bullet to Bullhorn: Stories of Advocacy, Activism and Hope*.

He graciously extended an invitation for me to be a guest on his radio program and join the NGVAC board of directors, both of which I gratefully accepted.

Sadly, Elliot died in February 2024. His memory and actions are deeply felt and a loss for all those whose lives he might have saved.

It is heartwarming to acknowledge that my relationship with Elliot continues with Elissa.

I recall Elliot always saying to me, "I am going to find Michael. I don't know where and I don't know when, but I am going to find him."

If an afterlife exists, perhaps they have reunited and are continuing their efforts in good work and justice.

MY FRIENDSHIP WITH RUTH BADER GINSBURG

"Fight for the things you care about but do it in a way that will lead others to join you."
~ *RBG*

Improbably, one of the most meaningful relationships of my life started with a women's tea.

While many erudite articles and books have been written by and about Justice Ruth Bader Ginsburg, I would like to share my own personal connections with her.

It was in the early fall of 1957. David and I were married only two months prior, and I was now the wife of a second year Harvard Law School student.

Shortly after our arrival in Cambridge, and before classes began, I received an invitation to a women's tea for the wives of the men enrolled at Harvard Law School. The tea's invitation was sent by the wife of the law school dean Erwin Griswold.

It was an exciting invitation and one which I was eager to

accept. The possibility of meeting other wives intrigued me, and I very much looked forward to the occasion.

I arrived at the event to find the room filled with the students' wives and very quickly struck up a conversation with one of them. While we were talking, I noticed a beautiful woman arrive at the tea with a basket on her arm. In that basket was a baby. That was Ruth Bader Ginsburg (and that baby is now a law school professor).

Ruth had been invited to the tea as a wife, although both she and her husband, Marty were Harvard Law School students. In 1957, there were only nine women who were admitted to the law school. Ruth was one of them.

David and Ruth were not in the same sections; however, I knew who she was and had much admiration for how she managed the demands of marriage, motherhood and matriculation as a woman in the law school.

Some years after graduation, David and I attended a law school reunion. Ruth and Marty were present. Marty had become a world- renowned tax-law attorney and a celebrated chef. The book he wrote on tax law is still used as a teaching tool to this day.

At the reunion, David and I connected with Ruth and Marty during the cocktail hour. When dinner was served, Marty invited us to sit with the two of them. I still revel in the memories of that evening. Ruth was quiet and soft spoken. Marty was not. He had a great sense of humor and regaled us with countless stories that had us doubled over in laughter.

Ruth and I communicated periodically during the ensuing years. It was a joy to send her a congratulatory note after each of her judicial appointments starting with her first when President Carter had appointed her to serve as a judge on the U.S.

Court of Appeals for the District of Columbia in Washington, D.C.

You can imagine the elation we felt after President Clinton appointed Ruth to the Supreme Court. In an especially jubilant way, we acknowledged her success and as always received a warm response in return.

Over the years, Ruth's compassion became evident for others and the law, which showed itself in the opinions she handed down as a justice.

That same compassion was demonstrated to David and me after she learned of our personal tragedy.

I had published my first book, *"The Unthinkable: Life, Loss and a Mother's Mission to Ban Illegal Guns."* The purpose of the book was to tell a personal story about gun violence and to reach out to others who had experienced the same tragedies.

One day, David asked me, "Have you told Ruth what happened? She would want to know."

I told him I was reluctant to share such sad news with her. David urged me to change my mind, and I did. I wrote to Ruth and sent her a copy of my book. I received the following note from her:

> "I didn't know of the incomprehensible sadness you and David live with. It is a fitting tribute that you have told your story, one that should move legions. It is equally laudable that you are devoting your life to the cause of keeping guns out of the hands of people who should not have them. Wishing you continuing courage in that life-saving endeavor.
>
> With applause and affection,
>
> Ruth"

There are several incidents that keep reverberating within my brain pertaining to my friendship with Ruth that have resulted in other friendships.

For example, I vividly remember a phone call from her in which she shared the happy news. "Lois," she said, speaking with an elation in her voice that was contagious. "just a quick call. My nephew, Daniel Stiepleman has written a screenplay. The title is, "On the Basis of Sex." I have read it and think it is quite good. It is about a tax code case Marty and I argued together."

David and I were somewhat familiar with this case, having learned about it in the many books that were written about her. The screenplay offers a comprehensive examination of a trusting marriage, a visually striking working relationship, and the effective resolution of two significant legal issues: the tax code and gender equality.

After Ruth's passing, I wrote to Daniel to express my condolences and to relay his aunt's pride in his work. It is gratifying to note that Daniel and I have developed a relationship and that he has warmly acknowledged my reaching out to him about the woman he so beautifully refers to as his "Justice Aunt Ruth."

Another occurrence came about as the fortuitous result of an unexpected change of plans.

On a Saturday, in the Fall of 2017, I was supposed to travel by bus from where I live on Long Island to attend a MOMS DEMAND ACTION gun safety rally in Washington D.C. The bus was scheduled to leave Long Island at 4:30 A.M.

I called Ruth's office and spoke to her bright, capable assistant, Lauren Stanley, to say I was going to be in Washington, and how much I would enjoy seeing Ruth while I was there. Lauren shared Ruth's schedule with me, and I said I would contact Ruth at some point.

That prior Friday night, I learned that the bus trip had been canceled. Only three people had signed up, making the excursion too costly for the company to provide the transportation.

I tried to reach Ruth, but it was too late. I left messages as to the change of plans, hoping the messages would be received.

With the trip canceled, I had accepted an invitation to speak at a local gun-safety rally on that same Saturday.

Upon returning home from the rally, I found a phone message from Ruth: "Where are you?"

Apparently, my messages had not been received.

Ultimately, Ruth and I spoke, and her response was: "I was concerned and wanted to be sure you were all right."

Yet, one more example of Ruth's compassion for others.

In still another instance, I was again scheduled to be in Washington on Monday, October 7, 2019. I knew that the day and date were special. It was the first Monday in October and the annual opening of the Supreme Court.

When Ruth heard of my imminent visit, she planned an exciting day. She invited me to sit in on the Court's opening arguments, and to receive a guided tour of the building conducted by one of her assistants. To top it off, Ruth invited me for a chat later in her chambers.

It was a day I shall never forget.

I witnessed, firsthand, the legal process in our Supreme Court. While I had recollections of seeing the magnificent court building before, the personal tour was eye-opening because I saw and learned much about the building that would not have been possible in a group.

Most extraordinary of all was our one-on-one conversation in Ruth's chambers, which included the special opportunity to learn about the arguments that had been presented earlier that day and to catch up on our respective lives.

While we were talking, Ruth asked, "Do you have a copy of Marty's cookbook?"

I replied in the negative.

As mentioned, Marty's reputation as a chef was impressive and widespread. He was renowned for cooking for dinner parties for the other justices and their spouses.

Without hesitation, Ruth jumped up from the chair in which she was sitting and ran into the office where her assistants worked.

"Please get Marty's cookbook," she said. "I want to give Lois a copy."

One of Ruth's assistants immediately brought out a copy and gave it to her.

Ruth sat down and signed it, "For David."

I have prepared some of Marty's recipes, not only because they are delicious, but also as a means to honor the memories of both Marty and Ruth.

Additionally, over the years, my friendship with Lauren has become most meaningful, both for her kindness and her connection to the Ginsburgs.

It was a joy to learn about Lauren's family and the birth of her second child.

During the summer of 2023, I realized I had not communicated with Lauren for several months. So, I sent Lauren an email.

I received an immediate response from Lauren with shocking news. Her husband, a young man, only 33 years old had suddenly developed an incurable illness and passed away in February 2023.

Saddened, I picked up the phone and called Lauren to extend my condolences. "Why didn't you tell me?" I asked.

Through her tears, Lauren said, "I hesitated to tell you because I didn't know what to say, and I know you are no stranger to loss."

"I'm so sorry," I said. "Please do not feel that way. I regard myself as a survivor, and as a survivor, I think I can help you, which in fact, also gives me strength."

Speaking with Lauren made me think of Ruth as well. She was a survivor with insurmountable strength. The day after Marty's passing in 2010, she was on the Court's bench because she was determined to issue her opinion in a major case in person.

Ruth's friend, the noted journalist, Nina Totenberg wrote of Ruth's explanation as to why she appeared while in mourning, "Marty would have wanted it this way."

My reflections of Ruth are manifold. My life was enriched knowing her as a friend and a role model. She still lives on through all she accomplished for humanity and is now the source for the connections to her assistant, Lauren, and her nephew, Daniel. They are both infinitely appreciated for their compassion for others and their compassion to me.

18

RABBI SUSAN TALVE

"Compassion is an action word with no boundaries."
~ *Prince*

In considering the great artist Prince's wise words, I think immediately of Rabbi Susan Talve and the deep humanitarianism that is the hallmark of both the woman and her rabbinate. Over the years, I have come to consider Rabbi Talve as the embodiment of wisdom, compassion and belief in the worth of all humankind.

I had heard much that was praiseworthy about the rabbi from my daughter Susan long before I had the good fortune to meet her.

Little did I know just how meaningful my connection to the rabbi would become.

That connection took place in a variety of ways including our shared activism, our surprise regarding the rabbi's aunt and sadly, the loss of our beloved daughters.

Susie grew up in Great Neck, New York. She moved to St. Louis in the early '90s with her three children before she was divorced. She was especially drawn to Rabbi Talve's social activism because it was similar to the milieu she had experienced in the liberally focused Great Neck community while she was growing up.

I vividly recall a conversation I had with Susie after she had become an admirer of the rabbi. "Ma, the next time you and Dad visit St. Louis, you must come with me to listen to Susan Talve at her synagogue, Central Reform Congregation. She is an amazing person, and her sermons are riveting. And like you, she is an activist."

Indeed, we did attend a Rosh Hashanah service at Central Reform during one of our visits. Susie was absolutely correct. With its emphasis on the inclusiveness of all humanity, Rabbi Talve's sermon was enormously inspiring.

As I learned that day and confirmed in the years to come, one only has to be in the company of the rabbi to be awed by her vibrancy and kindness. You immediately feel enveloped with warmth in conversation with her.

Rabbi Talve is deeply committed to inclusivity whether it be fostering civil liberties, combating racism and antisemitism or offering support for the LGBTQIA community.

Under the rabbi's leadership, Central Reform serves as a congregational site for the African American and LGBTQIA communities: a safe place for those who have been victims of racial or social inequities. It came as no surprise to learn that Rabbi Talve and Central Reform are a beacon for the progressive Jewish community in St. Louis.

To cite two examples: In the early '80s Rabbi Talve began marrying same-gender couples, and her compassion for the Black Lives Matter movement was palpable after Michael Brown's killing in Ferguson, Missouri.

My personal connection to Rabbi Talve came about after Susie was shot in December 2008 by a teenaged burglar in possession of a stolen handgun.

My book, *"The Unthinkable: Life, Loss and a Mother's Mission to Ban Illegal Guns,"* was published in 2013. The purpose of the book was to tell the story of my daughter, an accomplished young woman and devoted mother of three, who finally realized her dream of opening her own fitness studio just months before she was so cruelly killed.

Given Rabbi Talve's activism against violence, I was connected to her by a mutual friend who knew of our commonality in the fight for gun safety. Consequently, in December 2015 she invited me to speak at her synagogue about my story and activism regarding gun-safety measures.

I was deeply touched by Rabbi Talve's sensitivity to my family's loss and to the campaign for gun safety that I was forging. It was a response that resonates with me to this day. While David did not have the same personal connection to the rabbi, nevertheless, he was Susie's father, and I shared my innermost feelings with him about the enormous comfort I felt being in the rabbi's company.

It was following my presentation at Central Reform that Rabbi Talve told me about her aunt Molly, who was a resident in a senior-living facility, coincidentally located close to my home in Great Neck.

It was my pleasure to spend time with Molly and, resultant to that, to further cement the rabbi's and my relationship.

My connection to Rabbi Talve and her husband, Rabbi James Goodman, deepened after I learned that they also suffered the loss of their daughter, Adina Talve Goodman, who was only 31 years old.

While Adina's loss was different from ours, still it was the loss of a child.

Our hearts went out to them.

All I could think of was two grieving rabbis, and a major aspect of their profession is to give comfort to those who mourn. I hoped to be of help in whatever way possible, particularly as it applied to our similar losses.

It was within that framework that my connection with Rabbi Talve became truly meaningful.

I learned that Adina was born with a congenital heart condition. She survived multiple medical procedures including a heart transplant when she was nineteen. Her health was further compromised after she was diagnosed with cancer.

Adina was a people person who, like her parents, was a humanitarian. She was also a published author whose book, *"Your Hearts, Your Scars,"* is a profound compilation of essays regarding her medical ordeals. Upon reading the book, I was immediately struck by the uncommon wisdom in its pages that belied Adina's young age.

The rabbi and I are two mothers who suffered the untimely deaths of our daughters. We live with that similar pain.

Several years passed. Rabbi Talve and I had never really had the opportunity to share our thoughts regarding our daughters' losses. In November 2024, David and I flew to St. Louis for a weekend visit with our grandchildren. The trip turned out to be the perfect occasion for us as mothers to have a heart-to-heart conversation.

Our time together was heartwarming and relevant. Rabbi Talve said, "I do what I do to help others so Adina would be proud of me."

I looked at the rabbi in surprise. "Your actions to help others are because that is who you are, it is in your makeup."

The rabbi paused and seemed to be in deep thought.

"Yes," I continued, "Adina would be proud of you because you have gone above and beyond what any human being would do to reach out to those who are needy, in your social activism both as a rabbi and a human being."

"I miss her," she said.

"I know how you feel."

Rabbi Talve sat in silence for a moment, and I said, "I try to emphasize what I have, not what I don't have."

"I agree," she replied.

"And the one thing I bless is having David."

Rabbi Talve immediately replied, "Jim is my rock."

"Susan," I said, "we are fortunate to have husbands who are loving, supportive and sensitive. I know of instances where some couples' marriages disintegrate after the loss of a child."

"I know of instances like that as well."

"It's sad."

We looked at one another, our bodies emotionally charged but with the strongest feelings of connection, and a bond that was most comforting for us both.

I will always remember that conversation with Rabbi Talve. It initiated a deeper relationship between us as parents and friends than ever.

My connection with Rabbis Talve and Goodman, exemplary role models for all those whose lives they have touched, including David's and mine, is a source of inestimable meaning in my life.

19

JILL SCHUPP

I am only one, but still I am one. I cannot do everything, but still I can do something, and because I cannot do everything, I will not refuse to do something that I can do. What I can do, I should do. And what I should do, by the grace of God, I will do.
~ *Edward Everett Hale*

The foregoing quotation is indicative of Jill Schupp's compassion. Although I knew Jill Schupp's name, it would be several years before I met her when our paths would cross in a very special way.

Initially, I had learned about her from Susie, who displayed a lawn sign when Schupp was a candidate for the Missouri House of Representatives. Upon winning the election, she served as a Democratic member of that body representing St. Louis County's 82nd, then 88th district from 2009 to 2014.

As a public official, Schupp possessed exemplary credentials. Her political career began in 2000 as a member of the school board in Ladue, a suburb of St. Louis, where she served for six years including two terms as board president. In 2007, she was elected to the city council of Creve Coeur, another St. Louis suburb.

After serving in the House, Schupp won election to the State Senate where she served from 2014 to 2022. However, her political career came to an end when she lost to the Republican incumbent, Ann Wagner, in the race for a Missouri congressional seat in 2020.

It was while offering support for Schupp's State House candidate that Susie learned she and Schupp both were members of the same synagogue.

It is that connection and its impact on my life that I reflect on and wish to share.

Just prior to the 2020 election, I came across some campaign literature about Schupp, who was then a member of the Missouri Senate and the Democratic candidate for the contested congressional seat.

As I was familiar with her name and Susie's past support, I sent Schupp a note praising her efforts in the state capital and gladly included a campaign contribution toward her congressional bid.

In the note, I explained who I was and that I wished to support her for a variety of reasons including her stellar history working for social justice and Susie's wholehearted past support. I trusted my daughter's judgment and wanted to act accordingly. It was also a means to keep Susie's memory alive.

To my surprise, Jill Schupp called me several weeks later to thank me for the contribution and to share her story about the night Susie was killed as well as her own personal story regarding gun violence.

That night the police and an EMS unit were at Susie's home trying to revive her, to no avail. Two of her children, Sarah and Daniel, were there with Alvin Glazier, Susie's partner, all distraughtly waiting while the EMS was working on her. Tragically, Susie's life could not be saved. EMS took her body to the morgue, and simultaneously, the police expressed the necessity to interview Sarah, Daniel and Alvin at the police station regarding any information they could share.

At the police station, my grandchildren had the presence of mind to call someone who knew their family for support and solace. That person turned out to be the cantor from their synagogue, of which Schupp was also a member.

During our call, Schupp told me she happened to be at the police station that same night to attend a meeting and spotted the temple's cantor as she was leaving.

She knew immediately something was wrong from the cantor's demeanor, but she didn't know what it was. She said he looked forlorn, upset, burdened by shock and disbelief. It wasn't until several hours later that she learned the devastating news.

She said, "It was unfathomable, and particularly for me because it reawakened horrific visions of my brother being shot."

Taken aback, I said, "I'm so sorry."

"Thank you," she said. "This is what I remember. My brother, Garry Seltzer, is a lawyer. In 1992 he acted as the attorney for Kenneth Baumruk in a contentious divorce case. Baumruk was also known to be volatile."

"What happened?" I asked.

"It was awful. He went on a shooting rampage in the St. Louis County Courthouse. In the courtroom, he opened his briefcase, pulled out two pistols and shot the judge, the other attorney, the bailiff, my brother and his soon-to-be-ex-wife, who died. She was the only fatality."

"Thank goodness, your brother survived as well as the others who were shot."

"Yes, Garry was shot three times. Baumruk was a madman with a lot of hate."

"What happened to Baumruk?"

"He was shot nine times by the police but survived. There were two trials. The first was declared a mistrial because it was held in the courtroom where the shooting took place. He was found guilty during the second trial and eventually died in prison."

"Jill, thank you for sharing this information with me."

"You're welcome. I had to because of my personal experience, just to let you know that I understand, and that my heart goes out to you."

Those grave, yet heartfelt, conversations with Jill initiated a connection that continues to have meaning in my life to this day.

When we spoke, I shared the fact that I was in the process of completing my book, *From Bullet to Bullhorn: Stories of Advocacy, Activism and Hope,* and asked for her endorsement. Graciously, she kindly accepted my request. Her endorsement was written both as an elected official, and more important, as a concerned human being dedicated to saving lives, not endangering them. She wrote:

> *Policies in my state and our nation ignore the link between easy access to guns and the act of violence that quashes a human life and leaves survivors' lives forever changed. "From Bullet to Bullhorn" shares the devastating reality of death by gun violence through heart-wrenching real stories that bring the shock, the pain, the holes in the heart that also irrevocably change the lives of the survivors. The book brings to life the stories of death that otherwise have become so common that a 'sending thoughts and prayers' response allows those unaffected to go back to their lives...until the next ubiquitous and senseless attack touches the previously untouched. Share the stories, work for policies, and vote for those who share your voice.*

Although we live in different states, which precludes a daily personal connection, nevertheless, Jill's presence resounds in my mind and heart for her infinite kindness.

During her years of public service, she gave of herself as an elected official and as a human being to support my family and me in our time of loss and in support of all humanity.

20

THE HEALER

"Success is not final, failure is not fatal, it is the courage to continue that counts."
~ Winston Churchill

Fight the good fight.

There are people in this world whose philosophy and actions go above and beyond for the preservation of humanity.

In St. Louis, Dr. LJ Punch is the embodiment of that maxim.

Dr. Martin Luther King, Jr. said, "Life's most persistent and urgent question is: "What are you doing for others?"

Doing for others is Dr. Punch's mantra which he combines with impressive credentials. Dr. Punch is a pianist, a podcaster, a poet, an activist and a world-renowned trauma surgeon. He received his undergraduate degree from Yale University and his medical training at the University of Connecticut School of Medicine.

Professionally, Dr. Punch is a critical care surgeon, a former associate professor of surgery and a scholar at the Institute for Public Health at Washington University School of Medicine in St. Louis.

From an early age Dr. Punch was captured by the merits of discipline and making people's lives better, culturally and professionally. Culturally, that discipline manifested itself with piano lessons given to him by a Mrs. Carter in Wellsville, Ohio, the small town in which he lived. Those piano lessons provided him with the opportunity to play for the enjoyment of others. Professionally, as a highly skilled trauma surgeon his deep sense of discipline was the key to saving lives. In essence, he "soaked up" a kind and creative philosophy, a "give and take," that Mrs. Carter termed, "radical generosity." In other words, employing knowledge and resources to improve the lives of all the people he touched.

Since then, his activism has put into practice the heartfelt values he holds for the health and wellbeing of people in his St. Louis community. St. Louis is a hotbed of violence. Guns are readily accessible. In his work, Dr. Punch has emphasized the prevalence of shootings as a health-related issue. Additionally, he has addressed the issue as an enormous moral and medical problem and has been a fierce advocate for active prevention to help those who are affected.

Sir Winston Churchill said, "We make a living by what we get. We make a life of what we give."

It can almost be said that Dr. Punch's life is all about giving, so much so that it might seem there are simultaneously two Dr. Punch's one that gives of his medical healing and one who gives of his heart.

Dr. Punch's work is primarily in trauma settings particularly as it applies to the epidemic of gun violence in St. Louis.

It was in that capacity that I was first introduced to Dr. Punch when I was invited to speak at a gun safety event at the Institute for Public Health at Washington University in 2017 after I had published my first book, *The Unthinkable: Life, Loss and a Mother's Mission to Ban Illegal Guns* regarding our daughter's murder in St. Louis.

At that time, Dr. Punch was teaching at the university and was a staff surgeon at Barnes Hospital. The audience at this event was comprised of many people including social workers, physicians, psychologists, members of the community and medical students.

It became immediately clear to me the admiration and respect Dr. Punch received from his students. I overheard part of a conversation two students were engaged in. "You'd better check that out with Punch because you know he's a stickler for accuracy."

I later learned of his expertise as a trauma surgeon. It was said of him that he could remove bullets that the ordinary surgeon would not be able to touch.

I saw Dr. Punch a second time at another St. Louis gun safety event. David and I were visiting our family in St. Louis, and I was looking forward to attending this meeting. Our plan was for David to drop me off at the event and for me to take a taxi back to our hotel at the event's conclusion.

When the meeting was over, I stood in the lobby of the building and was speaking on the phone to a taxi service to take me back to the hotel. Upon hearing my conversation with the taxi service, Dr. Punch immediately said, "Come, I'll take you. I have enough time to drop you off and get back to the hospital."

What ensued was a ride I shall never forget.

We shared our thoughts about "doing for the next guy,"--- helping where we could.

During the ride, I kept thinking, I was in the presence of greatness and of a person who was rightfully called "an angel of the streets."

While driving, Dr. Punch listened with intensity to the story of my involvement regarding gun safety measures. I explained that I began as an advocate and then became an activist after my daughter, Susie's murder by a teenage burglar in possession of a stolen handgun.

Thoughtfully, Dr. Punch asked, "Are you bitter?"

My reply was, "Saddened, yes, Bitter, no. I could be, but I am not. I cannot walk around blaming our society for my loss. They were just two misguided teenagers. I love people and I am going to lose the very people I want to keep close if I walk around complaining. It is not going to bring Susie back."

He quickly answered, "I agree and love people as well. That's why I went into medicine as a career."

During the ride, Dr. Punch's compassion was deeply felt in a strong human-to-human sense. He shared his ideas for fighting the life-threatening issue of gun violence as a trauma surgeon.

Like a laser beam, his activism zeroes in the crusade against violence and specifically gun violence as his life-saving mission.

As a surgeon, Dr. Punch began the Stop the Bleed initiative at the T. a "hands-on" psychological and medical anti-violence counseling center located in midtown St. Louis. It is actively involved in saving people "at risk," such as drug-abusers and providing support for bullet related injuries.

Regarding the gun violence issue and knowing that someone can bleed out in one minute, while an ambulance can take fifteen-minutes to arrive, Dr. Punch began educating students and adults at the T to empower them with training and skills to save a life should a shooting occur. To date, he has taught this life-saving technique to over 10,000 people in the St. Louis metropolitan area.

Over the years, Dr. Punch became frustrated with conventional healthcare treatment and began to fight gun violence with a holistic approach. That led him to resigning from Barnes Hospital and founded BRIC, the Bullet Related Injury Clinic.

BRIC is unique in its focus. It addresses the needs of the disadvantaged, those who are most affected by gunshot wounds and who can least afford traditional health care methods. The program, which is free, focuses solely on the individual—no papers needing signing, no insurance plans needing to be owned.

The purpose of the program is to bridge potentially fatal gaps in order to care for people who have been threatened or injured by bullets but also goes far beyond those immediate needs with aftercare for those who have been affected by a shooting. It includes addressing the emotional, social, mental and spiritual suffering of a gun related trauma. The far-reaching philosophy of BRIC speaks volumes about Dr. Punch's humanism. The program also includes counseling for those who have either been threatened by gun violence or lost a loved one due to a shooting.

Dr. Punch demonstrates his many interests in a variety of ways, such as his love of music and as a poet.

I vividly remember receiving a phone call from Dr. Punch. It was an invitation to a reading in St. Louis of poems that Dr. Punch had written.

Unfortunately, I could not attend as we were home in New York. However, Dr. Punch graciously sent one of his poems to me which is included below. His invitation was touching as was his thoughtfulness to send the poem to me. It emphasized the kindness and depth of a special person whom I consider to be a gift to those who believe in and seek out the best in people.

12 inches,
they told her.
That would be the size of the incision
to free her body.
She thought,
I'll never have children.
"What's that?"
she said,
pointing to her abdomen
beside her umbilicus,
the historical home of her umbilical cord,
the place where her mother gave her life.
And as her mother stood there beside her, proud,
hiding her own wounds.
She would have put it the umbilical cord back
in that moment
to give her daughter life
again.

Anything for her child...
In this place
now
A little piece of death
reminded her baby
that
SHE
WAS
NOT
SAFE.
"It's important
and it hurts

and they sent me home with a piece of paper and a bag of gauze
and it's all I can think about
everyday."

She got it.
She knew what a bullet in her belly meant.
She knew what it could do to the life she wanted
to give
through her own baby's umbilical cord,
to her essence
that would be
one day.

Three generations were in the clinic room with me that day.

An iPhone
and some gel
made a shadow of sound
and there it was,
right where she said it was
where the doctors said it couldn't be.
Then their 12 inches became
2 miles down the way became
20 minutes in my clinic room became
a half inch - then OUT,
and I lifted the kryptonite from her body,
free.

They say
bullets go into bodies but I say
bullets go into lives and once they get there
we've got to take them out.
We've got to get them out.

We've got to get the lead out.
We've got to.
We've got…
We have
what we need.
We could get the lead out.

The bullet wasn't even that deep.

21

WHAT GOES AROUND COMES AROUND

"Life is the art of drawing without an eraser"
~ *John Gardner*

D avid and I gave my mother a plate for her eightieth birthday. The plate shined like sterling silver, but it was made of an aluminum alloy that only resembled that silvery metal.

We were attracted to the plate, not because it looked like sterling silver but for the inspiring inscription written on the outer rim: "Health, love, wealth, and time to enjoy them."

Those words attracted us and were what we wished for my mother and for people everywhere.

I called it "the good luck plate," because health, love, wealth and the presence of those qualities can be viewed in three categories: to strive for them, to know when you possess them and to appreciate the luck that you have them.

While health, love and wealth may each seem to be marked by straightforward meanings, in fact, they mean more than what appears at first blush. Wealth, for example, does not only mean monetary wealth. Ralph Waldo Emerson and Virgil expressed the identical sentiment: "The greatest wealth is health." A sense of wellbeing is included in this usage. The same can be said about "love," a concept not necessarily limited in meaning to romantic love.

Rabbi Nachman of Breslov said, "Let the good in me connect with the good in others until all the world is transformed through the compelling power of love."

Also, regarding the subject of love and its inclusiveness, Dr. Martin Luther King Jr. said, "I believe that unarmed truth and unconditional love will have the final word in reality."

In essence, Rabbi Nachman's and Dr. King's statements emphasize that love powers a profound connection to the human experience, one far from limited to the romantic definition of the word. It is a connection that represents a human quality that we must aspire to and take contentment in when it is achieved.

The following narrative exemplifies the beauty of the power of love and the wealth of friendship.

Madge Kaplan was a friend of my mother, David and me. In fact, over the course of the more than thirty years we knew Madge, she became more than just a friend. We considered her to be part of our family and celebrated many special occasions with her, such as birthdays, anniversaries and holidays.

Madge always admired my mother's décor and was especially attracted to the silver plate.

We were fortunate to have had my mother until she was ninety-eight years old. She was an amazing woman, with an active mind, a great sense of humor and a love of reading. She also had a weak frame caused by osteoporosis, which meant she could easily suffer fractured bones. Fortunately, we were blessed to have wonderful caregivers to help her. I used to say to her, "Mom, your mind gallops, but your legs don't."

After her passing, I was going to distribute her belongings to people she had known and cared for and those who had cared for her. The remainder, I was going to donate to charity.

David and I asked Madge if she would like to have anything of my mother's as a keepsake.

"Yes," she said, "I would love to have the silver plate."

So, we passed the plate on to Madge.

Sadly, Madge died several years later.

After the funeral, her daughter was distributing some of her mother's items in the same manner that David and I had given away Mom's items.

She asked, "Is there anything you would like to have of my mother's?"

"Yes," I said, "I would love to have the silver plate."

Recently, my good friend Bev Zeldin died. At ninety-seven, she was a spirited lady but was diagnosed with an aggressive cancer.

Her children had spoken to me about donating Bev's furnishings after her passing.

"This is so meaningful to me," I said. "I would like to tell you a story," the same story I am sharing with you, dear reader.

As things stand, under circumstances I can only think of as "good karma," I now own three beautiful paintings that were in Bev's home and Mom's silver plate.

With the passage of time, that plate has taken on a life of its own. Through the years, I have bought that same plate for others to acknowledge a milestone, such as a birthday or anniversary. And I share its history with them regarding my mother and Madge. In turn, that history has often sparked a reflection for those who have received the plate.

Two friends shared their story with me after I had given the plate to them to celebrate their anniversary. They explained that they were hosting a dinner party at their home. Their guests admired the plate. Whereupon the hosts said, "We would like to tell you the story about the person who gave us that plate."

The existence of the plate has become a never-ending and engaging chronicle.

The presence of Mom's plate and Bev's three paintings evoke wonderful thoughts of people and experiences that were of special significance in my life and that stimulate warm memories for David and me. The keepsakes also represent the spirit and appreciation of reflections that can shape and inspire a life.

22

THE CIRCLE OF LIFE

"Whatever affects one directly, affects all indirectly. We must walk on in the days ahead with the audacious faith in the future.
~ *Rev. Martin Luther King, Jr.*

The Brazilian philosopher, Paulo Freire wrote, "Learning is a process where knowledge is presented to us, then shaped through understanding, discussion and reflection."

The preceding essays highlight special moments in my life. The essays describe experiences that shaped important aspects of my future understanding. They are representative of ensuing actions, sense of sharing and the awareness of the value of those special moments of dialogue and discussion.

Additionally, writing about special moments was a means to connect with others and perhaps share similarities regarding life experiences. In turn, the thought was for the reader to consider their own special experiences to share with others.

One might even loosely term such a process of reflecting and its influence on the future as "paying it forward." In other words, whether sharing your experiences can influence others.

Some of the stories illustrate humorous experiences, others are filled with pathos, and still others highlight the knowledge I acquired due to my association with skilled individuals in various fields.

Ultimately, writing about those experiences was a blending of the past, acknowledging the present and thoughts for the future. The project added another dimension to my life and was vitally affirming.

Over time I have learned that experiences, reflections and memories are deeply ingrained within our identity and are skintight.

All of these stories illustrate how life experiences can often reverberate full circle, and for the reader to consider whether sharing their experiences can have a positive influence or provide assistance to others.

ACKNOWLEDGMENTS

Stephanie Larkin of Red Penguin Books deserves accolades for her exceptional creativity, encouragement and support fostering both a strong professional relationship and personal connection. Special thanks to editors Katherine Abraham and Janet Larkin for their careful attention to detail and insightful guidance throughout the process.

I am equally grateful to Richard Lowenstein of AllWrite Consulting for his unwavering patience and dedication to this project. His efforts have contributed significantly to making this work meaningful. His association is a blessing.

Acknowledgment must also be made to Debbie Heicklen for her gracious instruction with her adept computer skills.

Many thanks to Ruth Karter and Gladys Roth for listening as this manuscript evolved and sharing their insightful suggestions.

AUTHOR'S NOTE

During a working meeting with my publisher, Stephanie Larkin, astutely observed that my manuscript consisted of twenty-two essays. She said, "numerologically speaking, that number has special significance. I think you should conduct a little investigation and write an author's note that includes your rationale for writing this book."

Her intriguing comment prompted me to follow her suggestion. In the process, I acquired valuable knowledge that I am eager to share with all readers.

Pythygoras, the ancient mathematician and father of numerology said, "Everything is numbers and to know numbers is to know thyself."

Symbolic key components of numbers include unity, duality, harmony, balance, spiritual and mystical meaning. Stability, misfortune, transformation and freedom are also key elements to consider.

Numerical meanings hold special significance culturally and biblically in Western and Eastern beliefs. For example, on the one hand, the number eighteen in the Jewish religion symbolizes life, as in the word, "chai," resulting in the phrase "L'chayim," which translates "to life."

On the other hand, the Chinese regard the number four as unlucky due to its phonetic resemblance to the word for death.

In Western culture and particularly in the United States, the number thirteen is regarded with fear. As a result, buildings often skip the thirteenth floor, and people avoid events on Friday the 13th.

The number twenty-two is often referred to as the "Master Builder," or the "Master Teacher." There are three numbers that are regarded as Master Builders: eleven, twenty-two and thirty-three. But twenty-two is viewed as the most powerful because it represents unified inner strength and leadership.

As I kept writing, unknowingly perhaps, I was striving to reach that number to emphasize a correlation between my experiences and encounters with others and the possible relationship with numerological significance.

Inspired by numerology, I explored the symbolism of the number twenty-two. By delving deeper, it became apparent that my collection of essays was not merely a random assembly but rather a harmonious compilation underscored by the profound essence of this number. The essays reflect themes of unity and duality, balance and transformation, all while weaving together a tapestry that mirrors the multifaceted nature of human experiences.

As I explored the intricate meanings associated with twenty-two, I discovered they are believed to embody the essence of practicality and idealism, bridging the gap between the material and the spiritual realms. This resonated deeply with my own journey in writing these essays, as each piece serves as a testament to my encounters with the world, both seen and unseen.

The realization that my work aligns with the significance of twenty-two filled me with a sense of purpose and validation. It was as though the universe had subtly guided me to achieve this milestone, infusing my writing with a hidden layer of meaning that transcends the ordinary.

ALSO BY LOIS SCHAFFER

The Unthinkable:
Life, Loss and a Mother's Mission to Ban Illegal Guns

From Bullet to Bullhorn:
Stories of Advocacy, Action and Hope

www.ingramcontent.com/pod-product-compliance
Lightning Source LLC
Chambersburg PA
CBHW061748070526
44585CB00025B/2835